Symbolic Insult in Diplomacy

Diplomacy and Foreign Policy

Volumes published in this Brill Research Perspectives title are listed at *brill.com/rpdf*

Symbolic Insult in Diplomacy

A Subtle Game of Diplomatic Slap

By

Alisher Faizullaev

BRILL
NIJHOFF

LEIDEN | BOSTON

This paperback book edition is simultaneously published as issue 2.4 (2017) of *Diplomacy and Foreign Policy*, DOI 10.1163/24056006-12340008.

Library of Congress Control Number: 2018931187

Typeface for the Latin, Greek, and Cyrillic scripts: "Brill". See and download: brill.com/brill-typeface.

ISBN 978-90-04-35411-1 (paperback)
ISBN 978-90-04-35414-2 (e-book)

This book is printed on acid-free paper and produced in a sustainable manner.

Contents

Symbolic Insult in Diplomacy

A Subtle Game of Diplomatic Slap

Alisher Faizullaev
The University of World Economy and Diplomacy, Uzbekistan
alisher@faizullaev.com

Abstract

This paper approaches symbolic insult in diplomacy as the use of symbolic means by states to oppress the opponent's sense of Self, to hurt its self-esteem and social status in order to achieve their foreign policy objectives, or as a reaction to a threat from Other. The paper posits that diplomatic actors are extremely sensitive to Self related matters, and may use such sensitivity for influencing each other, bargaining over the issues of importance, and simply defending their sense of Self while they confront the opponent. The enormous importance of collective Self in diplomacy may instigate a variety of social strategic games, including tacit and deceptive ones. The diplomatic actor's acute sensitivity to recognition, honor and social status sharpens its sense of Self, which makes any humiliation painful. Therefore, protection of self-regard, dignity and public face becomes a critical issue in diplomatic practice. At the same time, that makes the diplomatic actor's Self vulnerable, and provides the opposing Other opportunities for manipulation and symbolic abuse.

The paper argues that symbolic insult in diplomacy occurs in a highly normative environment, and depends on political objectives, shared knowledge, social perception and practices, and can negatively affect relationships between diplomatic actors, the opponent's self-perception, self-feeling and security of Self—ontological security. I distinguish three forms of symbolic insult used in diplomacy: by misrecognition ("diplomatic bypassing"), direct confrontation ("diplomatic punch") and concealed verbal or nonverbal actions ("diplomatic slap"). The paper focuses on the third, indirect form, or "diplomatic slap" which employs obscure symbolic insults as a means of tacit manipulation for influencing the opponent, or as an instrument of restoring social status.

By highlighting interest-based (political), value-based (moral), relationship-based (social) and right-based (legal) imperatives of international diplomacy, this paper shows that diplomatic actors can use symbolically expressed but subtle "slap" for

 | DOI 10.1163/9789004354142_002

balancing their interests and relationships in dealing with the opponent: Tacit or implicit symbolic insult usually appears ambiguous which may allow the offender to promote its interests but also to stay engaged with the victim.

Keywords

symbolic insult – humiliation – diplomacy – international politics – imperatives – manipulations – Self and Other

Introduction: The Puzzle of Symbolic Insult in Diplomacy[1]

The word "diplomacy" is usually associated with politeness, courtesy, civility and searching for peace among nations. A diplomatic method of conflict resolution points to peacefulness, understanding and accord. Indeed, diplomacy and peace are intertwined concepts, and diplomatic relations, contacts, negotiations and arrangements play a significant role in international peacebuilding. Diplomacy can fulfill such a noble mission only when it helps nations to communicate with each other and understand one another. Thus, truthfulness,

1 The first version of this paper was presented to the Section "Symbolic Violence in Diplomatic Practice" of the 9th Pan-European Conference on International Relations held in 23–26 November, 2015 in Giardini Naxos, Sicily, Italy (2015). I would like to thank Professor Corneliu Bjola of Oxford University who invited me to co-organize and co-chair this section together with him. The conference section, its panels and roundtable discussions helped to develop the ideas of this paper, and I am grateful to the participants. I also appreciate those who participated and discussed my paper when I presented it in the Global Governance and Diplomacy Public Speaker Series at the Oxford Department of International Development on October 16, 2017.

This work could not have been written without my Fulbright scholarship at the Fletcher School of Law and Diplomacy, Tufts University and the Institute for the Study of Diplomacy, School of Foreign Service, Georgetown University in 2011–12, as well as a fellowship at the Center for International Peace and Security Studies at McGill University in 2014, and I would like to thank Professors Eileen Babbitt of Tufts University, Paula Newberg of Georgetown University and Vincent Pouliot of McGill University for their support and collaboration.

I also would like to express my gratitude to the editors of the Brill Research Perspectives in Diplomacy and Foreign Policy for their insightful suggestions as well as the anonymous reviewers whose critique and recommendations helped to improve the manuscript. I am thankful for Professors Corneliu Bjola, Noé Cornago, Jérémie Cornut, Jörg Friedrichs, Vincent Pouliot and Reinhard Wolf for their valuable comments.

honesty, respect and goodwill are essential for the spirit of diplomacy and for diplomatic practices.

However, diplomacy cannot only be sincere, honest and respectful in dealing with counterparts but can also employ manipulative, deceptive and tricky communication. This happens when it serves the foreign policy objectives of a diplomatic actor—the state.[2] In other words, diplomacy can use concealed and disingenuous methods—*diplomatic tricks or manipulations*—as part of a political agenda or as an instrument for achieving political goals.

Diplomacy does not boil down to trickery. In fact, diplomatic tricks have been the subject to scrutiny mostly in the media while scholarly literature on diplomacy has generally ignored this phenomenon. I think there are two main reasons for this lack of attention. First, it is very difficult to detect and conceptualize the hidden game of diplomatic manipulations because that is a subtle reality of diplomacy. Therefore, the media, which can afford to be more speculative, is able to discuss this elusive aspect of diplomatic games more. Second, the dominant concept of diplomacy, namely "peaceful way of resolving conflicts" or "instrument of international cooperation," does not align with the ideas of hidden intrigues and tricks. Although diplomatic intrigues, conspiracies and tricks may be primarily associated with the palace diplomacy of the past, many people, even those outside of diplomatic circles, still tend to believe that diplomats often cheat, or, at least, can play some political games with double—exposed and veiled—meanings for the sake of their strategic objectives, or for defending "national interests". It is no wonder that Sir Henry Wotton's (1568–1639) statement "An ambassador is an honest gentleman sent to lie abroad for the good of his country" is still cited so often.

Subtlety and ambiguity of symbolic insult in diplomacy poses challenges for both diplomatic actors and observers: its existing hard to grasp, and its meaning, intention and effect difficult to comprehend. But as any insult, symbolic insult in diplomacy is a socially constructed phenomenon, and alongside with possibilities for different interpretation of it, there is a common sense which helps to catch its occurrence.

Scholarly works on "constructive ambiguity" of diplomatic signaling (Jönsson and Aggestam 1999; Cohen 1981) point to a very important role of polysemantic communication in diplomacy. To be flexible and overcome direct confrontations, diplomats often need to use polysemantic communication which allows for multiple interpretations. Diplomatic communiques and joint statements, in contrast to agreements and treaties, may use words and phrases that can be interpreted in different ways. However, that doesn't prevent

2 This paper focuses on interstate diplomacy.

diplomats from perfectly understanding each other (Langholtz 2004). Because diplomats do not always need to be direct in their communication and interaction, their understanding, receiving and sending a meaning of information is critically important for their professional activities. As any other meaningful human activity, diplomacy can only be based on shared knowledge and jointly constructed meanings. However, unlike many other forms of human activity, the art of diplomacy is grounded on the ability to construct both clear and obscure meanings. Concealed forms of symbolic insult in diplomacy are based on politically driven "destructive ambiguity" of diplomatic signaling.

This paper analyzes the use of abusive signaling or insulting communication as part of a hidden diplomatic game, or a social game of diplomacy. When trying to influence each other, diplomatic actors can exploit both positive and negative *strokes*, using Eric Berne's (1964) terminology. The paper explains this deviant behavior in diplomacy through the analysis of a collision between the diplomatic actors' interest-based (political) and relationship-based (social, or relational) imperatives. In other words, symbolic insult in diplomacy serves the achieving political objectives of the insulter while keeping its normative relationships or engagement with the humiliated actor or victim.

Berne studied "games people play" where individuals enter social intercourse at both open and hidden levels. For him, a stroke is a fundamental unit of social action and recognition. Berne's theory is psychological and analyzes social interactions at an individual, or interpersonal level. This paper concentrates on diplomatic intercourse and focuses on symbolic interactions between or among states as collective actors. It shows that diplomatic actors, through their individual representatives, can use concealed negative stroking—so called diplomatic slaps or snubs to influence each other. I approach symbolic insult in diplomacy as a manipulative action, or political trickery. Unlike manipulative games between people with their individual Selves though, diplomatic subtle and insulting games take place by and around collective Selves related to states. Because of the importance and vulnerability of a collective Self represented by diplomats, it may be much more sensitive to insults and humiliations than an individual Self. So, symbolic insult in diplomacy needs to be really subtle in order to be truly diplomatic.

International diplomacy uses symbolism extensively (Adler-Nissen 2013; Bull 2012; Cohen 1987; Der Derian 1987b; Faizullaev 2013; O'Neill 2002; Pouliot 2010; Sharp 2009; Watson 1982). The significance of diplomatic symbols and symbolic interactions, such as rituals and ceremonies, is related to the representational nature of diplomacy (Sharp 1999) and communicative power of symbolism in a social and political context. "Diplomacy is the conduct of international relations by persons who are official agents; hence the importance of diplomacy of letters of credence or other tokens of representative or symbolic status" (Bull 2012: 157). Symbols and symbolic actions carry out meaning that senders and receivers need to understand, so both interacting sides participate in the meaning making process. Actors who participate in symbolic exchange or interaction, socially construct the process and outcome.

Diplomats and diplomatic missions abroad embody the state, and they inevitably represent the state politically, legally and symbolically. By entering symbolic interaction, for example, participating in ceremonies or official meetings, diplomatic actors are involved in the meaning making process. Sometimes in diplomacy, just a short meeting between antagonists—even without any results—may have a huge and far-reaching significance. This is because of the important symbolic meaning of that meeting.

States are not presented in human senses (Wendt 1999), and their behavior and intentions can be expressed and comprehended symbolically (Faizullaev 2013). Symbols and symbolic interactions help diplomats and the wider audience to capture the meaning of international affairs, and create a shared knowledge about diplomatic events, intercourses and intentions. Symbolism is essential for diplomatic practice and communication between international actors (Jönsson and Hall 2005). Diplomacy requires tact, delicate and refined communication, and symbolic interaction is an effective means of doing so. In short, to be flexible and meaningful, diplomacy needs symbolic communication and interaction.

Diplomacy may exploit different kinds of symbolic supports and rewards as well as abuses and assaults. Recognition, acknowledgement, appreciation, praise, tributes, high level visits and meetings, official dinners and gift exchanges, guard of honor and gang salutes, and the awarding of medals and honorary degrees are among positive symbolic gestures or credits that diplomatic actors can offer each other. However, diplomacy can also be aggressive, offensive, antagonistic, hostile, coercive and manipulative. International diplomacy is a peaceful activity but it may use different forms of insult to overcome or oppose the opponent and achieve foreign policy objectives. Because of the representational nature of diplomacy, any diplomatic kindness and affront carries some symbolic meaning.

This paper argues that diplomatic actors can employ elusive but symbolically significant forms of debasing the opponent as a manipulative act to abuse the opponent's sense of Self. Such a weakening of the opponent can help the insulter to advance its strategic interests while maintaining a certain level of relationship with the humiliated. But symbolic insult can also provide the humiliated side with some interpretational opportunities that may allow them to save face and continue the relationship with the insulter, or to return a symbolic offense. Even weak states or non-state actors can use symbolic insults against powerful states.[3] Nowadays it is easier to symbolically insult through the media, Internet and digital diplomacy. Hurting someone by the fake news and propaganda did not appear in our time, but modern technology contributed to the unprecedented spread of this phenomenon. Gross insults are rare in diplomatic practice, because diplomacy is supposed to contain civility and tact. Nonetheless, nowadays diplomatic actors may use subtle or symbolic insult more frequently to affect the opponent's ontological security and integrity.

The notion of symbolic insult is close to the concept of *symbolic violence* developed by Pierre Bourdieu. He introduced the concepts of symbolic capital, symbolic power and symbolic violence, and the latter presented an instrument and form of social, economic or cultural dominance. Bourdieu primarily paid attention to the symbolic dimension of domination in a society, to the mechanisms of acquiring, maintaining and using symbolic capital and symbolic power as well as applying symbolic violence for domination when other, more apparent means, are not applicable. Bourdieu defined symbolic violence as "the gentle, invisible form of violence, which is never recognized as such", and this "hidden exploitation is the form taken by man's exploitation of man whenever overt, brutal exploitation is impossible" (1977: 192). That form of domination "is only exerted through the communication in which it is disguised" (1977: 237). According to Bourdieu, symbolic violence becomes a "natural" order through the internalization of existing social domination. However, symbolic violence can be used not only by a socially recognized stronger side against a weaker member of a society but also by the latter against the former. Thus, as Bourdieu pointed out, women can use "soft violence, sometimes almost invisible", "against the physical or symbolic violence of men" (2001: 32).

Despite the proximity between the concepts of symbolic violence and symbolic insult—both point to the role of symbolism in producing concealed and meaningful harm. In this paper, I do not follow the footsteps of Bourdieu:

3 Insult and humiliation can take place not only in diplomacy among states, but also in relations between state and non-state actors. Both state and non-state actors can act as insulters or to be victims. For example, the terrorist attacks on September 11, 2001 which were committed by a group—a non-state actor—were not just a physical assault on the United States but also a symbolic insult against the most powerful nation in the world. As well, the images of the Abu Ghraib prison torture and prisoners' abuse insulted many Muslim and non-Muslim societies; cartoons insulting Prophet Muhammad insulted Muslims all over the world and instigated a diplomatic crisis is another example (see the related works of Lene Hansen 2011 and 2015). In asymmetric conflicts, the failure to retaliate may humiliate both the strong and weak sides (McCauley 2017: 255), and post 9/11 American global policy was affected by dynamics of humiliation (Saurette 2006: 495).

I argue, that in diplomacy, an object of symbolic insult is the diplomatic actors' sense of Self. Bourdieu didn't use the concept of Self or sense of Self, and for him symbolic violence was not an intentional act. In Bourdieu's theory, the concept of symbolic violence is closely linked with his other fundamental concepts such as practice, habitus, field, capital and doxa. In contrast, this paper approaches symbolic insult in diplomacy as a symbolic means for diplomatic actors to obscurely oppress or hurt their opponent's sense of Self in order to achieve their foreign policy objectives or as a reaction to a threat from the Other. In other words, it is a subtle social game between Self and Other in an international political context where the oneness, integrity and social status of the actor is at stake. In this respect, humiliating the diplomatic actor's sense of Self means jeopardizing its ontological security.

The paper starts from "The Case of President Trump and Prime Minister Marković interaction: Was it a Diplomatic Insult?" This case study helps to underline some important aspects of symbolic insult in diplomacy related to ambiguity of diplomatic signaling, differences between diplomatic and public perceptions of the international hierarchy, the role of interpretations, emotions and strategic relations in the assessment of assimmetric social interactions in diplomacy.

Next two sections, "Diplomatic Actors: Self and Other" and "Diplomatic Actor's Sense of Self and Ontological Security" analyze the nature of the diplomatic actor, relationship between Self and Other in international diplomacy, and the role of sense of Self, self-regard, honor and social status. As diplomatic actors, states enter international social relationships at various levels and different degrees of openness and honesty to protect their interests, identities, sense of Self and ontological securities.

In "Three Types of Insult in Diplomacy", I distinguish various types of insulting actions and interactions that diplomatic actors may commit in social interaction between Self and Other. The paper focuses on subtle but symbolically significant insults in diplomacy which I describe as "diplomatic slap".

The next section, "Diplomatic Imperatives and Symbolic Insult", discusses the political, moral, social and legal essentials or driving forces of international diplomacy, and their role in the emergence of symbolically insulting behavior. The paper argues that Self can make a diplomatic slap in the face of Other because of its interest-based and relationship-based imperatives clash while they are still maintaining and balancing their normative relationships with each other.

The following section, "Symbolic Insult in Diplomacy as a Manipulative Practice", analyzes the hidden game of calculated manipulations in diplomacy. Diplomatic stratagems, media, digital and representational manipulations are among the topics I explore.

In the subsequent part, "Symbolic Insult in Digital Diplomacy", I analyze the influence of modern informational technologies, particularly social media as a tool of diplomatic symbolic insult. The paper shows that diplomatic actors can be easily engaged in a "Twitter war" because of their involvement in the game around very sensitive public Selves.

"The Range and Level of Symbolic insult in Diplomacy", discusses the scope of symbolic insult in diplomacy, diplomatic insults at high-level diplomacy, and the role of symbolic gestures as both humiliating and healing practices in international diplomatic practice.

The section entitled "Tacit Bargaining and Symbolic Insult" is largely built on Thomas Schelling's theory of tacit and explicit bargaining. Distinguishing explicit negotiation and tacit bargaining in diplomacy, I argue that because of the mostly unarranged, implicit and flexible character of international bargaining, elusive symbolic offence is more often employed in the hidden bargaining process than in explicitly organized negotiations.

The next part, "Face Diplomacy and Symbolic Insult", uses Ervin Goffman's insights on face-work in relation to international diplomacy. The section studies "face-diplomacy" as a delicate social practice, and examines the use of symbolic insult between strategic rivals engaged in diplomatic face-work that usually takes place in public.

The final section "Handshake Diplomacy and Symbolic Insult" represents a case study of some symbolic interactions between President of France Emmanuel Macron and American President Donald Trump. It analyzes relations between body language, international pecking order and symbolic insult in high-level diplomatic interactions.

The paper presents various historical and recent cases while paying special attention to the Soviet-American and Russian-American confrontational relations. My objective is to better understand whether symbolic insults hinder or instigate physical confrontation between major nuclear powers. In my opinion, hostile symbolic interactions can work in both directions—provoking or neutralizing a real clash. In a growing conflict situation, any insult can lead to escalation. However, in a situation when parties run the risk of losing more than winning, and they desire to save face, a symbolic insult can also allow them to limit it with a "small quarrel". In other words, sometimes symbolic insult appears to be the lesser of two evils.

The Case of the President Trump and Prime Minister Marković Interaction: Was It a Diplomatic Insult?

During the North Atlantic Treaty Organization summit in Brussels in 2017, President Trump pushed aside Prime Minister of Montenegro Duško Marković to stand in front of head of states and governments of NATO member states. "Trump reaches out his right arm, grabs Markovic's right shoulder and pushes him aside. Markovic looks surprised. Trump doesn't acknowledge his existence as he moves past him. It's as if Markovic isn't there" (Schmidt 2017). "Instead of being insulted, he took the opportunity to thank Mr Trump for supporting Montenegro's membership in NATO" (ABC News 2017 a).

As Samantha Schmidt noted, "in fact, 'shove' was probably the most common word used to describe the fleeting, at best awkward interaction between Trump, the leader of the most powerful nation on Earth, and Dusko Markovic, the leader of Montenegro, a small Balkan nation of 600,000 attending its first summit as a NATO member after a nine-year accession process" (2017). Indeed, here are some related news headlines: "Donald Trump shoves fellow Nato leader, the Montenegro PM, aside" (Telegraph Reporters 2017), "Breaking down Trump's 'shove'" (Schmidt 2017), "Montenegro's prime minister didn't mind President Trump's shove seen round the world" (Link 2017), "Support floods in for Montenegro PM after Trump shove" (Kroet 2017), "Trump Shove on Montenegro's Leader Draws Balkan Media Ire" (Savic 2017), "President Trump shoved the Montenegro prime minister at NATO" (Estepa 2017), "Donald Trump: Did the President just shove aside a prime minister?" (ABC News a), "Opponents of Montenegro Joining NATO Seize on Trump Shoving Incident" (Radio Free Europe/Radio Liberty 2017), "The Shove Heard Round the World" (Glasser 2017), and "Little Montenegro Muscles Way Into NATO, Despite Trump Shove" (Siemaszko 2017).

We can look at this incident from different perspectives. From Marcović perspective, everything was quite all right. He didn't dramatize the incident and tried positively portray the happening. "This was an inoffensive situation", he said. "I do not see it in any other way" (Schmidt 2017). According to Marcović, it was "only a harmless incident," "had nothing to do with him personally and did not even merit an apology" (Glasser 2017). Marković also noted that he had the opportunity to thank Donald Trump personally for his support of Montenegro's entry into NATO and "of course the further development of our bilateral relations" (Schmidt 2017). Marković said "that it is natural for the president of the United States to be in the first row" (Schmidt 2017). Obviously, Marković wanted to calm down unnecessary emotions around this incident. He told German newspaper Die Bild "that he did not believe Trump intended to push him aside in order to move to the front of a group of leaders for photographs", and "it was a completely harmless event" (Kroet 2017). In an interview to Politico Magazine, Marković said: "I have to say that I'm very grateful that this incident, so to say, took place. Because this is what made us so famous," and "This is what made Montenegro so famous" (Glasser 2017).

White House spokesman Sean Spicer also did not inflate the situation and pointed to the predetermined spots for the "family photo" for which the leaders were going "implying that Trump was not trying to get a better position" (Schmidt 2017). President Trump didn't comment the incident.

But the "people of Montenegro were not amused"; Montenegro newspaper Vijesti wrote that "it seems Donald Trump did not want that anyone overshadows his presence at the summit", and some Balkan websites blared the headlines such as "America First" and "Where do you think you are going?" (Siemaszko 2017).

> "America First!" cried one CNN affiliate in the region, while Montenegro's Vijesti newspaper said Trump purposely "removed" Markovic to hog the limelight. In neighboring Serbia, the Alo tabloid called the move "brutal," with the Blic newspaper claiming Trump wanted to "show who's in charge."
>
> Milan Knezevic, leader of Montenegro's opposition and anti-NATO Democratic People's Party, said by phone that Trump's behavior "is clear proof that there's no such thing as equality in NATO", showing that the country is just a "smudge" on the alliance's map.
>
> SAVIC AND KUZMANOVIC 2017

Here is another the Montenegro opposition party representative's opinion:

> "Dusko Markovic has banged on for years about Montenegro becoming a NATO member ... which will be respected and will be at the table where decisions are taken," said Jovan Vucurovic, spokesman for the opposition Democratic Front.
>
> "Well, now we've seen just what the president of a world power thinks of that," he said, adding, "The problem isn't what Trump did ... It's the fact that Markovic excused it and humbly sought to justify" Trump's aggressive behavior.
>
> RADIO FREE EUROPE/RADIO LIBERTY 2017

Glasser (2017) mentioned Marković's reaction to the opinion of those who oppose the NATO membership inside his country: "It is their belief, actually, that this harmless event took place in Brussels will slow down Montenegro and it would harm Montenegro as a NATO member state". Marković dismissed this position as "nonsensical" (Glasser 2017).

What happened in Brussels was widely discussed in the media and social media. After that incident, Prime Minister Marković received thousands of emails and messages of support from U.S. and EU citizens (Kroet 2017). But according the Russian state news agency TASS, "Internet audience in Montenegro is furious with the row at NATO's summit over the incident between US President Donald Trump and their country's Prime Minister Dusko Markovic. Some authors of commentaries on the news about the incident, posted on the portal of Montenegro's national television RTCG, urge sanctions against the US" (2017 b). TASS referred to "one user" who urged to impose "tough sanctions against America to let it know whose prime minster was pushed and humiliated" (2017 b). And even more: "The RTCG said that a sign-up campaign had allegedly begun in the United States in support of the demand for making Trump apologize, but the headline had no proof in the news story" (TASS News Agency 2017 b). This, according to TASS, "merely added to the Montenegrins' anger", who believe that "everything happened that way because somebody wished to take an undeserved place and play an utterly undeserved role" (2017 b).

Some celebrities also reacted to this incident. For example, the Harry Potter author J. K. Rowling (2017) put on her Twitter account the video footage of the Trump-Marković interaction and remarked: "You tiny, tiny, tiny little man".[4]

Many newspaper and social media publications about this incident contained various emotions, but there were some attempts to analyze it at a deeper political level. Here is Susan Glasser's analysis:

> Because the president of the United States had in fact blundered into the most symbolic target possible: The leader of a tiny Balkan country that had chosen, at significant risk to itself, to join the NATO alliance—even as Trump became the first American leader since World War II to publicly question the alliance's mission, future relevance and even its core principle of collective defense. Trump may not have meant it, but with one push he inadvertently highlighted not only his own ambivalence about the alliance but the tribulations of many countries in Eastern Europe that, like Montenegro, believe they are increasingly in the cross hairs of Russia.
>
> GLASSER 2017

So, does this case of "shove diplomacy" point to a diplomatic insult? It is much easier to admit an insult when it happens deliberately, openly and rudely. But it is harder to grasp insult when it takes place ambiguously. However, as this paper will show, diplomats sometimes use the elusive, subtle, obscure forms of insult in interactions with each other. As we saw above, the judgment about

4 By October 25, 2017, the tweet got 439,509 likes, 212,689 retweets and 18,000 replies.

the existence or non-existence of a more hidden type of insult would depend on the interests, attitudes and positions of the actors and observers, on the social, moral and legal norms within which one assesses the incident. Usually we regard insult as a deliberate action is aimed at harming or putting down someone. When the same kind of action is done accidentally, we typically tend to speak about embarrassing situation or embarrassment. We can also refer to humiliation when the injured party experiences negative feelings because of the insult. So, to accurately grasp and assess any incident, we need to better understand the situation, and the motives of participants and those who valuate the happening. Our assessment would also depend on our ability to consider various strategic and situational factors affecting the incident/insult.

At a NATO summit President Trump and Prime Minister Marković acted as the highest diplomats of their countries. And that incident—a physical assertion of dominance in a diplomatic setting—can demonstrate the difference between an individual diplomat's sense of place and the public perception of social inequality in diplomacy. An individual diplomat who participate in these kinds of situations can express his or her opinion by taking into consideration both political and relationship imperatives, but public opinion is more affected by emotions and collective sense of Self. In other words, the diplomatic world and the public one may react to symbolic inequality or international pecking order differently. But in some situations, diplomats can be more sensitive to any sings of symbolic abuse of their sense of Self and dignity, and react more acutely than the public. Diplomats and a wider audience can see the situation similarly too, or the public opinion may be divided. Diplomats' reaction to insulting or embarrassing situations may vary depending on whether they happened publicly or privately. In short, diplomatic agents act and interact in a complex and often dynamic political, social, moral and legal structure and need to consider many factors in their behavior including public opinion at home and abroad. Sometimes but not always they can significantly shape this structure. By interacting with each other and a wider public, diplomats participate in a social construction of their reality and act as meaning-makers. This also applies to the construction and understanding of diplomatic insults: insult in diplomacy is an intersubjective phenomenon. In diplomacy, coding and decoding of the offensive behavior occur within diplomatic setting and under the influence of diplomatic legal and social norms. So, understanding diplomatic culture and norms is essential for analyzing not only brutal violations of diplomatic etiquette but also subtler, i.e. "diplomatic" breach of them.

The Trump-Marković interaction case shows the role and importance of interpretation of diplomatic interactions and signaling, various—including tacit—factors and aspects of meaning-making in diplomacy. Even a brief look at this incident demonstrates its complexity and relations with many political, strategic, social, psychological, legal and moral issues. For analyzing the episode, we can bring such matters as politics and psychology of a membership in international organization, pecking order in international relations and within international organizations, relationships between individuals and among states in international politics and diplomacy, in-group competition and solidarity, the actor-observer bias in international politics, legal and social equality/inequality of states and their official representatives, diplomatic protocol and permissibility of certain forms of interaction at high-level diplomacy, public perception of dominance/submissiveness in diplomatic setting, etc. For better understanding this case, apparently, we need to consider issues related to individual and collective sense of Self, diplomatic symbolism, reputation, image, respect, honor, national pride, dignity, tact and saving face in international politics and diplomacy. Obviously, such a comprehensive approach requires a large and interdisciplinary research. In this paper, I intend to use a social approach for understanding diplomatic insults because any insult, first of all, is a social phenomenon: it happens in social interaction, depends on relations between participants and affects their relationships. Social norms, social expectations and social perception do matter as well. The social approach can also help to better understand the role of political, legal and moral factors in diplomacy because any diplomatic practice is a social practice. The social study of diplomatic insult does not negate but complements other approaches to studying this phenomenon.

Diplomatic Actors: Self and Other

Essential parts of diplomatic history and practices are well recorded, but despite the extensive study, "diplomacy has been particularly resist to theory" (Der Derian 1987 a: 91). The recent advancement of diplomatic theory is mainly connected to different forms of social thinking, and students of international diplomacy are paying more attention to the area of social interactions, or sociality. "Diplomacy is, first of all, a social activity", said Ian Hurd (2015: 36). As Rebecca Adler-Nissen stated, "diplomacy should be understood as a social world of its own, abiding to its own rules, norms and codes of conduct" (2012: 4). By establishing diplomatic relations, international actors enter a specific type of social relations with their norms, rules, regulations, culture of interaction and influence.

Since diplomacy is a socially oriented activity, and social relationship between the involved parties is of crucial importance, scholars in diplomatic studies have always paid some attention to social factors. However, the social conceptualization of diplomacy differed since it depended on the attraction of the elements of social theories and approaches. The English School of International Relations represents one of the most notable approaches in this regard: it presented diplomacy as one of the key institutions of the international society as a global social complex (Suganami 2010), and studied diplomacy as a social phenomenon and social practice (Neumann 2002). As Hedley Bull, one of the key figures in this school, noticed, "diplomacy fulfils the function of symbolising the existence of the society of states" (2012: 166). Entering into this society means being part of certain social relations.

It is noteworthy, that the recent development of diplomatic theory represented in the works of Costas Constantinou (1996; 2010), James Der Derian (1987 a; 1987 b; 2010), Khrister Jönsson and Martin Hall (2005), Iver Neumann (2011; 2012; 2013), Vincent Pouliot (2010; 2011; 2016), Paul Sharp (2009), Chris Reus-Smith (1999), Rebecca Adler-Nissen (2012; 2013; 2014; 2015), Noé Cornago (2013), Corneliu Bjola (2013), Markus Holmes (2013) and Jérémie Cornut (2017) largely takes place within the variety of social approaches to diplomacy. These and other scholars, who consider diplomacy as a social practice, showed that diplomatic activities are not simply a function of political determinants or interests, but also are deeply connected to social relations, norms, rules, regulations and structures that have an essential impact on the conduct of international politics. Diplomacy is built into the international social system, and one of the main "fabrics" that constructs the structure of this system is "relationship" between the involved parties.

Considering diplomacy as a social practice, Sharp noted that social theorizing about diplomacy is important and helps us to understand it better (2013: 54). According to Jönsson and Hall, "Diplomatic recognition and socialization are the core mechanisms through which diplomacy helps constituting—and is, in turn, constituted by—any given differentiation of international space" (2005: 38). Diplomatic recognition itself represents a social phenomenon based on normative interactions of the parties as accountable intentional actors.

Modern diplomatic studies suggest insightful reflections on socializing disposition and mission of diplomacy (Constantinou and Der Derian 2010), socialization of adversary states into the international society of states through diplomatic relations (Wiseman 2010), the role of diplomacy in socialization of revolutionary states (Armstrong 1993), diplomacy's everyday social practices; socialization of states through the socialization of diplomats (Neumann 2011;

2012; 2013), and social order in multilateral diplomacy, or so called multilateral pecking order (Pouliot 2010; 2011; 2016). Recently published book on relational aspects of diplomacy edited by Ole Jacob Sending, Vincent Pouliot and Iver Neumann aims to "bring social theory to bear on diplomacy" (2015: 1).

The social dimension in diplomatic studies enriches the study of political, legal, economic and other aspects of diplomatic relations by taking into consideration such socially determined and meaningful factors as symbolic interaction, role behavior, shared ideas and norms, cultural patterns, identity formation, status building, hierarchical relations, in-group and out-group perceptions, attitudes and dispositions, and relationship between Self and Other(s). In short, this approach helps to reveal the essential features of diplomacy related to its fundamental—social nature.

Diplomacy is a civilized way of resolving conflicts and differences among social actors, "institutionalized interaction between polities" (Neumann 2012: 4). Diplomacy cannot exist without a specific diplomatic culture. The concept "diplomatic culture" points to some general social, cultural and legal norms related to the conduct of international diplomacy (Bull 2012; Dittmer and McConnel 2016; Sharp 2014). Although it is not a strictly defined term, such a culture is based on civility, respect, courteousness and willingness to overcome differences between parties, which socializes them into similar behavior (Zartman and Berman 1982: 226) and provides some safety in their interactions (Meerts 1999: 86). As Der Derian puts it, diplomacy is about mediation of "estrangement between human beings by symbolic power and social constraints" (1987 b: 42). Usually diplomacy is associated to relations between states as international actors. Indeed, only states can establish formal diplomatic relations and officially send each other diplomats—ambassadors and other diplomatic representatives. That is why the words "diplomacy" and "international diplomacy" appear as synonymous. Traditional diplomacy is diplomacy between states, or, to be more exact, between governments which represent states. Apparently, governments represent their states and conduct diplomacy through their own representations—government agencies such as foreign ministries and agents such as professional diplomats.

However, currently we are witnessing the emergence of new forms or types of diplomacy, for example, "public diplomacy" where a government of one country approaches the public of another country. Another trend is "Track II" diplomacy where nongovernmental organizations exercise diplomatic activities in relations with states and other non-state actors, or "citizen diplomacy" where individuals affect international relations and politics. We can also see how new state and non-state actors' aggregations have started to play a role in world affairs. Nowadays, scholars discuss "plural diplomacies" (Cornago 2013) "everyday diplomacy" (Sennet 2012: 211–246; Cornago 2013; Constantinou 2006; 2016) and "transprofessional diplomacy" (Constantinou, Cornago and McConnel 2016). Thus, modern concept of diplomacy is certainly developing.

In this paper, we are focusing on traditional—state-to-state—diplomacy. However, nowadays even traditional interstate diplomacy is going through rapid changes. It uses new practices such as digital diplomacy, and contemporary diplomats need to acquire new skills such as social media and social engagement skills and methods of quantitative analysis.

The ultimate actors of international diplomacy are still states. States establish diplomatic relations and enter into diplomatic intercourse. But states cannot speak to each other, sit around the table and negotiate with one another: in diplomacy, they should be represented by governments and governmental organizations—agencies, and individuals such as head of states and governments, foreign ministers and ambassadors, other diplomats and government officials—or agents. In other words, interstate diplomacy can be conducted by triune—actor-agency-agent—diplomatic entities: no actor can act without its agency and agent, no agency exists without actor and agent, and no agent can perform without actor and agency. The inseparability of state (actor), organization (agency) and individual (agent) means that efficient diplomacy requires diplomatic efficiency at all three levels: state, organization, and individual (Faizullaev 2014 a). In this paper, I often refer to "diplomatic actor" bearing in mind that the actor is represented by an agent, and the agent himself or herself conducts his or her activity with the organizational help of the agency.

The state is a multifaceted actor. It can act and interact as a diplomatic actor, or war actor, or trade actor, or cultural actor and so on. The state can also perform different roles simultaneously. As international actor, the state can combine its diplomatic, military, economic, cultural and other capacities. The state can be considered as a diplomatic actor when it uses diplomatic means, channels, culture and norms. So, the state as a diplomatic actor is narrower than the state as an international actor. However, the state as a diplomatic actor can also use a wider means, including military, trade and culture. In intergovernmental diplomacy, states interact through their official representatives. But official representatives can also use unofficial channels or private individuals in performing their job. Therefore, sometimes it might be difficult to clearly distinguish the roles the states play in their interactions and relationships with other international players. Nevertheless, when states engage in talk, negotiation, problem solving activities by using diplomatic means and norms, we can consider them as diplomatic actors.

The state is a purposive actor with a sense of Self (Wendt 1999: 194), "a real corporate being to which we can properly attribute human qualities like identities, interests, and intentionality" (Wendt 1999: 215). Diplomats represent the state's Self internationally (Faizullaev 2006), and any humiliation they experience becomes a social humiliation of those whose interests and identities they represent. However, not only diplomats but regular citizens can experience this so-called ambassadorial feeling—"the sojourner's perception of himself as a representative of his home country" (Torbiorn 1982: 114)—when they travel abroad or participate in an international sports tournament or cultural festival, or feel "banal nationalism" when they support national sports teams or face a threat to symbols of their country (Billing 1995). John F. Kennedy's words "Ask not what your country can do for you, ask what you can do for your country" may portray a model of relationships between individual Selves and a country's Self people need to serve, respect and protect. Such a collective Self, incidentally, emerges as a kind of grand or super Self.

Self is "a person's essential being that distinguishes them from others, especially considered as the object of introspection or reflexive action", "one's particular nature or personality; the qualities that make one individual or unique" (Oxford Dictionaries 2017). Self is a socially constructed phenomenon, and it emerges because of the actor's interactions with Other (Mead 1934). Self can exist only when Other exists, so Self and Other are interconnected and interdependent antagonists, and their interactions and relationship are essential for forming each side's identity and oneness. By interacting with Other(s), the actor shapes and develops its sense of Self.

According to George Mead (1934), the actor's Self has two aspects, or sides: "me" and "I": the former appears as an object, and the latter as a subject. In other words, "me" or "me-Self" represents the actor's self-consciousness, and "I" or "I-self" embodies its acting feature. So, Self, which contains I-ness and me-ness, can appear as a matter of identity and agency—social, corporate, individual, political, cultural or any other.

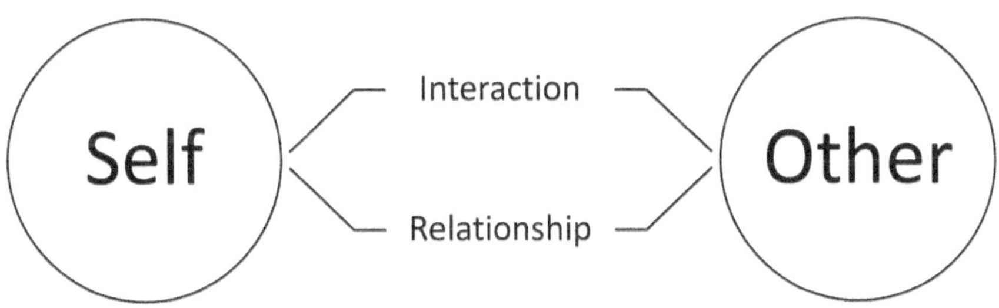

The concepts of Self and Other became significant parts of the identity and interaction discourse in international relation theory. Discussing collective identity formation in international relations, Neumann underlined the importance of the studying "Self/Other" nexus for a better understanding of the actors, "how they were constituted, how they maintain themselves, and under which preconditions they may be best studied by an examination of the margins of world politics" (1996: 168). Identities, as Wendt pointed out, "are constituted by both internal and external structures", and two kinds of ideas can enter into identity—"those held by the Self and those held by the Other" (1999: 224). Hansen rightly stated, that "foreign policy discourse always articulates a *Self* and a series of *Others*" (2006, 6). Self and Other are important concepts in understanding international relations and collective identity (Hall 2001), the state's ontological security (Bially Mattern 2005; Mitzen 2006; Steele 2008).

A narrative that Self tells of itself often appears as conceptualized identity, and that story has a strong relational component (Bjola and Kornprobst 2013: 123). As Bjola and Kornprobst pointed out, "The definition of Self requires situating oneself vis-à-vis others. Self positively identifies with some significant Others while it negatively identifies with others (and does so to different degrees)" (2013: 123). In a social world, Self and Other are doomed to cooperate and confront. However, as conscious and intentional entities, Self and Other can manage or try to regulate their relationships by undertaking primarily cooperative or competitive actions and interactions, or by combining them.

The concepts of Self and Other can be instrumental in studying social aspects of diplomacy. Constantinou (2006) offered an innovative approach to relations between Self and Other in diplomacy. Discussing "homo-diplomacy"—diplomacy's human dimension and also spiritual and transformative potential, he underlined that Other, for example ethnic and national, is a part of a wider single Self. The mission of human diplomacy "is not only, not just, the knowledge and control of the Other but fundamentally the knowledge of the Self and this knowledge of the Self as a more reflective means of dealing with and transforming relations with Others" (Constantinou 2006: 351). This paper focuses on the form of alienation of Self and Other in diplomacy by using symbolic insult. However, the analysis of this hostility practice as a part of international politics can be useful in overcoming it and developing the more positive forms of diplomacy Constantinou talked about.

Diplomacy appears as one of the tools of managing and regulating international relations and politics, and as an instrument of foreign policy, it can be used for protecting the diplomatic actor's sense of Self and affecting/influencing Other(s). Symbolic insult in diplomacy occurs when "I-ness" of the

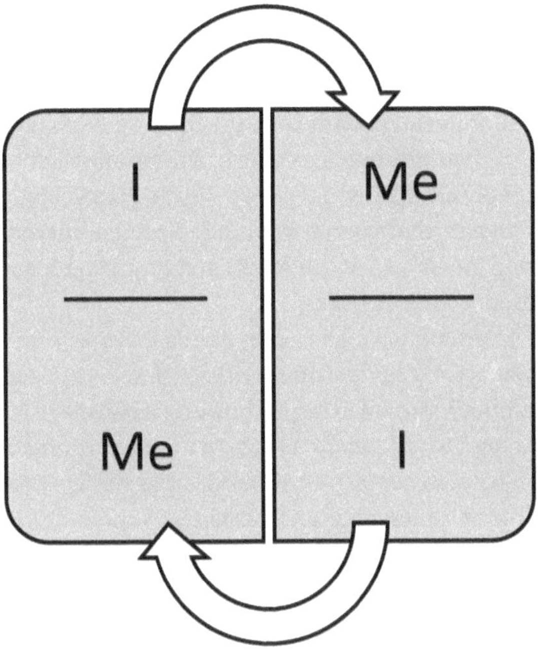

diplomatic actor uses symbolic interaction to hurt "me-ness" of the other actor. As a reaction, Other can actuate its "I-ness" to affront "me-ness" of the offender. That confrontational game of Selves may lead to the spiral of symbolic struggle aimed at infringement of diplomatic actors' sense of identity and oneness.

As Bially Mattern puts it, "the Self emerges through the culture/"realities" in which it is embedded" (2005: 599). Diplomatic actors bear their own national culture, but they also function within common diplomatic culture. Diplomatic culture is highly normative, status-sensitive and face-preserving. Honor, esteem, respect, dignity and public face are important elements of diplomacy and diplomatic culture. Diplomatic actors need to act and interact within established norms and diplomatic cultural patterns, by having high social status, self-regard and saving face as well as taking care of their interest, fundamental values and relationships. Such a highly normative and Self-sensitive environment may engender subtle and manipulative interaction between diplomatic actors through using symbolic means.

As Brian Hocking, Jan Melissen, Shaun Riordan and Paul Sharp remarked, diplomatic rules, conventions and norms have always been violated for the reason of policy but a strong enough commitment to them has existed in the past (2012: 27). This is no longer so because of the emergence of new international rules, conventions and norms as well as non-state actors engaged in the traditional diplomatic activities, blurring of the boundaries between internal and external affairs, demolishing diplomats' exclusive claim to authoritative representation, less effective protection of their traditional immunities and privileges (Hocking, Melissen, Riordan and Sharp 2012: 27). Modern diplomats are less blessed with the exceptional prestige inherent in their profession in the old days, and their traditionally elevated sense of Self became particularly vulnerable to the increased pressure that comes from the changing international environment and growing media and social media scrutiny. Diplomats' social eminency became exposed to greater risks.

Meerts (1999) noted that diplomats have lost their prerogatives as international negotiators: now they are in competition with civil servants and non-diplomat experts, and diplomacy turned to be just one of the players in interstate negotiations. In the modern world, relations between states are affected not just by diplomats but also representatives of many other professions, including politicians, journalists, businessmen and researchers; however in the increasingly international oriented world, the role of the diplomat as communicator, trusted agent and trouble-shooter will gain in significance (Meerts 1999). Indeed, despite the emergence of new international actors, diplomats officially represent their states—still the main international actors, and that imposes a large responsibility on them, sharpens their sense of Self related to the Self of their countries. Diplomatic skills may be related to "agency, advocacy, reporting, counseling, and stewardship" (Freeman 1997: 108), but the job requirements in the field of diplomacy become tougher. Modern diplomats need more social skills as well as digital proficiencies. And they should be more resistant to various kinds of stresses, including open and hidden threats and insults. Insult is an inevitable aspect of social relations (Korostelina 2014: 3). Ensuring physical, information and ontological security gained more importance in contemporary diplomacy.

Diplomatic Actor's Sense of Self and Ontological Security

Diplomacy as an international practice has its norms, rules and regulations developed throughout its long history. Coexistence, reciprocity (Jönsson and Hall 2005: 50) and civility (Sharp 2009: 205–206) are among fundamental social norms of diplomatic practice. Diplomatic conduct also relies on diplomatic protocol and etiquette—established and internationally accepted rules and habits. Another essential regulatory base of diplomatic practice is international law, particularly the Vienna Convention on Diplomatic Relations of 1961.

However, in some respects, international law and diplomatic protocol, on the one hand, and practice of diplomacy, on the other, may coexist in two separate dimensions without much interference with each other. We may refer to the equality of states and their authorized representatives in terms of international law and the norms of protocol, but at the same time to the real, practical inequality in international affairs and diplomatic practices based on actors' power and social status. This is exemplified through the existence of powerful and weak states, permanent members of the United Nations Security Council, international elite groups like G-7 and G-20, whose members may have a bigger influence in world politics and economy than smaller and relatively remote countries. States may have no equality in terms of their social status, reputation, attractiveness and international influence. Social and reputational inequality between countries can also be manifested in the status of individual diplomats. Often an ambassador from a large and wealthy country has more opportunities to access a host country's corridors of power than an ambassador from a less influential state.

The diplomatic sense of place is an essential characteristic of the practice of multilateral diplomacy (Pouliot 2016). In a Bourdieuvian sense, all these social orders of international relations and diplomacy generate symbolic power of the influential international actors, and to a large extent, international order is based on symbolic power relations. However, the existing symbolic power landscape of international politics provides opportunities for both powerful and weak states to use symbolically meaningful forms of tributes and affronts in their relations with each other. Weak or "rogue" states may employ a deliberative symbolic insult against their powerful opponents. Subtle symbolic insult can be used by both strong and weak Selves in countering both weak and strong Others without totally damaging the relationship, i.e. ambiguously and manipulatively.

Diplomacy attaches a great significance to the "precedence, or order of importance, of individual polities" (Jönsson and Hall 2005: 53). Diplomatic history has witnessed many conflicts over the precedence, and international diplomacy has developed various rules and practices to avoid such incidents. "Solemn entry", different countries' orders of precedence, official diplomatic lists, ceremonial and protocol principles and elaborations, conference rules of procedures are among them. However, the diplomatic actors' sensitivity to recognition, honor, respect and decent place among the peers makes the issue of precedence the Achilles heel of their Selves. Any violation of the sense of dignity and Self is perceived by the diplomatic actor as an inadmissible loss of social status or face, or even as a public shame which is difficult to tolerate.

"Shame produces a deep feeling of insecurity—it is a temporary but radical severance of a state's sense of Self", and states try to avoid this problem of ontological security at all costs (Steele 2008: 3).

Internationally, diplomats represent a collective or corporate Self of their states that is supposed to be greater than any individual human Self, and grander than the sum of the Selves of people who are the part of this unitary player. People tend to dignify such a paramount Self, partly through the disposal of symbols like national flags and emblems, performing a national anthem and etiquette related to it, and by using symbolic interactions such as ceremonies and rituals (Faizullaev 2006, 2007, 2013). People also legitimately attribute to this distinguished actor "anthropomorphic qualities like identities, interests, and intentionality" (Wendt 1999: 43). Eventually, such kind of an eminent and humanlike actor needs recognition, respect and honor—essential symbolic elements of diplomatic representation and intercourse. No diplomatic actor can exist and fulfil its functions without self-regard. However, where there is a sense of self-importance and a need for self-esteem, there might be a threat to them. Considering states as "actors" or "persons" with such properties as rationality, identities, interests and beliefs (Wendt 2004) assumes that one state-actor can respect and honor or deliberately insult and humiliate the other state-actor.

Scholars have paid considerable attention to the importance of recognition, respect, prestige, honor, dignity and face in international relations and politics (Morgenthau 1993; O'Neil 2001; Lebow 2008; Wolf 2011; Tsygankov 2012; Lindemann and Ringmar 2014; Paul, Larson and Wohlforth 2014; Friedrichs 2016; Renshon 2017, and others). However, most of these and related concepts which indicate certain socially defined characteristics of diplomacy have corresponding meanings and are often used interchangeably.[5] We may distinguish the following seven "social virtues" of diplomacy as a way of outlining an interrelated system of socially significant diplomatic merits: recognition,[6] status,[7]

5 Some of above mentioned concepts were comparatively analyzed by Reinhard Wolf (2011) in th context of international politics. Respect, according to Wolf, "is an attitude we expect others to show by the way they treat us" (2011: 112), honor is connected to "an actor's public reputation based on her public compliance with the code of a particular status group" (2011: 115), and dignity "delineates the core area of human worthiness as inter-subjectively defined by the prevailing culture" (2011: 116).

6 Related concepts: identification, validity, awareness, acknowledgment, acceptance and consideration. In diplomatic context, "recognition" may also be linked with the concepts of sovereignty and independence.

7 Related concepts: rank, eminence, prestige, prominence, importance, distinction, notability, power, reputation, significance and notoriety.

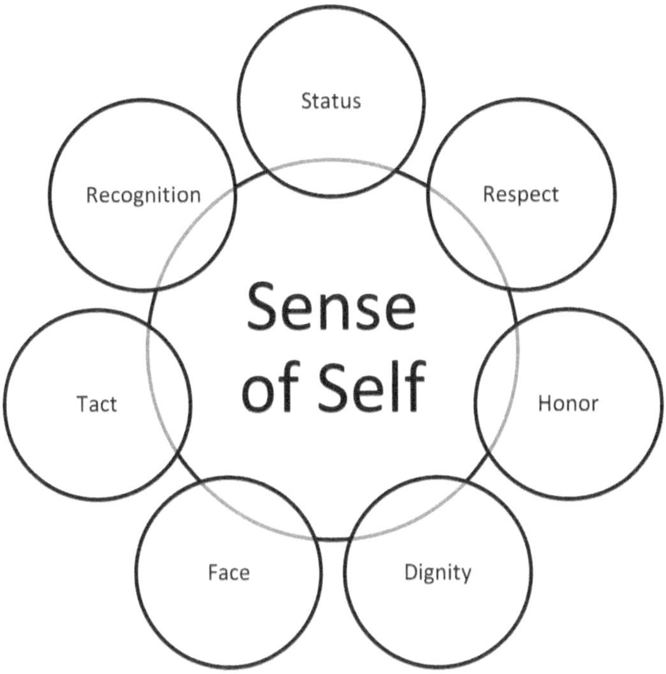

respect,[8] honor,[9] dignity,[10] face,[11] and tact.[12] The presence or absence of these social distinctions affect interactions and relationship between Self and Other in diplomacy, the diplomatic actor's sense of Self.

In this model, "recognition" points to the act of institution, "status"—to standing, "respect" and "honor"—to attitude,[13] "dignity"—to worth, "face"—to appearance, and "tact"—to conduct. The model characterizes the social culture of diplomacy and presumes that diplomatic actors recognize, respect and honor each other, possess themselves and acknowledge the other party's high status and dignity, take care of their own and the counterpart's face, and

8 Related concepts: regard, esteem, admiration and favor.
9 Related concepts: attention, pride, privilege and tribute.
10 Related concepts: worthiness, virtue, merit, decency and meaningfulness.
11 Related concepts: look, appearance, image and representation.
12 Related concepts: civility, finesse, delicacy, prudence, artfulness, sensitivity, discretion, good manners, politeness, appropriateness, propriety, courtesy, affability, gentility and etiquette.
13 Respect and honor are similar concepts, however the second tends to be more formal and symbolic, and used in a public setting (public honoring).

act/interact tactfully. In a real world of diplomacy, social factors interfere with political, economic, moral, ethical, legal, individual and other factors, and/or diplomats may have not enough social skills to perform above mentioned "social virtues" excellently. That means diplomatic actors may not always be good in recognizing, respecting, honoring and dignifying each other, acknowledging counterparts' status, helping them in saving face and behaving tactfully. But in diplomacy with its diplomatic social culture, lack of recognition, status, respect, honor, dignity, face and tact in relations with Other, or any sense of being non-recognized, disrespected, dishonored, undignified and treated tactlessly as well as insufficient acknowledgement of status and the loss of face may be perceived by Self as an insult. This can happen as a part of a social game of diplomacy with its subtle forms of communication.[14]

One of the closest to the concept of insult is "disrespect". Wolf (2011) approached respect/disrespect in international politics from the status recognition/misrecognition point of view. As he pointed out, "an actor feels disrespected when others—directly or by implication—lower her rank or question claims on which she grounds her status position—as she herself perceives it!", and "respectful behavior is experienced as an appropriate confirmation of one's rightful position, whereas acts of disrespect are seen as disregard for it" (2011: 107). Disrespect to our presence, as Wolf remarked, is closely related to "the various other forms of hurting our sense of importance" (2011: 111). Disrespect "is always seen as an unjustifiable denial of social rank, as a symbolic attack on an actor's self-perceived place in and meaning for society" (Wolf 2011: 116). In diplomacy, in my opinion, this is rather related to hurting of the actor's sense of Self but not just its social rank. In an international system

14 Hans Morgenthau pointed to the relations between diplomatic prestige and subtle strive for power. He introduced the concept "policy of prestige" and indicated by it "the subtle and intangible relationships" between international actors which are difficult to recognize "from the predominant theoretical and practical concern with the material aspect of power in the form of force, actual or threatened" (1993: 84). Morgenthau explained policy of prestige as one of the basic—although subtle and intangible—manifestations of the struggle for power on the international scene carried out primarily in the forms of diplomatic ceremonial and display of military force (1993: 84–98). We advance the argument that seeking prestige, recognition, honor and status on the international scene can be related not only to the struggle for power and advancement of interests through spectacular actions and interactions, as Morgenthau suggested, but also to the conception of Self in its confrontational relationships with the significant Other in more "ordinary" encounters such as diplomatic meetings, negotiations, conferences, public speeches, media and social media interventions. At that, the sense of Self can be related to the actor's political, moral, social and legal needs and aspirations.

with its pecking order, states may have their "sense of place", and their self-regard may not necessarily be connected with their sense of importance or social position. However, even with a moderate sense of social/international importance, the state may have an acute sense of Self. Of course, sense of Self depends in many ways on Others' attitudes toward Self, and how Others' treat the Self. But this sense is connected not only with the sense of importance as well as the senses of recognition, status, honor, prestige, dignity and face but also with the sense of existence: sense of Self, first of all, is an existential sense. Apart from all kinds of social attitudes and treatments coming from Others, the sense of Self is fueled by the sense of existence, and the sense of uniqueness. Obviously, the actor can experience its sense of existence and uniqueness not as a solipsist entity but in relations and interactions with other actors, i.e. as a social actor.

If we look at dictionaries, we can see that insult is usually defined in relation with an offensive or abusive remark or act, while disrespect is portrayed as a lack of respect. In other words, insult appears as a rude *action* upon someone, and disrespect may not be necessarily connected with *doing* something: on the contrary, it shows the absence of respectful treatment of someone. In a wider sense, this is also an action, but again, in case of disrespect the defining moment is the *lack* of some type of (respectful) behavior. But if disrespect looks as a deliberative *act* that hurts the actor's sense of Self, it turns to be an insult.

Diplomatic culture presupposes respectfulness: lack of respect as well as other "social virtues" of diplomacy, destroys the spirit of diplomacy. Therefore, in a usual diplomatic setting, diplomats are expected to demonstrate respectful, courteous and polite behavior. Obviously, diplomatic actors—because of their conflicting political objectives—may not truly respect each other, but showing disrespectful behavior toward others is considered undiplomatic. This is a part of social game of diplomacy. "Open denial of respect can severely harm an actor's reputation as a resolute defender of her interests" (Wolf 2011: 126). In short, in diplomacy, any demonstration of disrespect is seen as an insult.

Diplomatic actors need not only esteem but also self-esteem. For the social actor, esteem and self-esteem are inseparable because self-evaluation depends on the evaluation of Self by Others. However, there is also a certain reverse relationship between these phenomena: a high self-esteem or self-regard resulting from a high social status of Self, may affect the evaluation of Self by Others. In other words, the actor's high self-regard may—to a certain degree—uplift its social status and influence. Diplomatic actors need respect, social status and self-regard not just for their ego, but also for such a practical reason as influencing. Prestige, honor and other manifestations of social status expand the diplomatic actors' ability to influence, and make them more efficient. Thereby, a high self-esteem is a necessity in diplomatic intercourse.

Diplomatic tradition, culture and norms support the diplomatic actor's self-respect. The prestige of the diplomatic profession, the respectfulness of diplomatic language, the existence of diplomatic immunity, the glamour of diplomatic receptions, the splendor of diplomatic premises and chic of diplomatic cars all contribute to the sense of self-worthiness of diplomatic actors. According to Jörg Friedrichs (2016), not only individuals and groups but also states and nations have cultural differences in the pursuit of self-worth. "In some cultures, honor is the dominant pursuit. In others, saving face is the main concern. Yet, other cultures profess the primacy of human dignity" (Friedrichs 2016: 63). In other words, states and nations can relate to cultures of honor, face or dignity, and because of that, they seek self-worth differently. In addition, national cultures may affect states' international behavior. But when we discuss the behavior of states as diplomatic actors, we shall firstly consider diplomatic culture with its traditions, norms, written and unwritten rules. As well, diplomatic culture, as Friedrichs noted in our private conversation, comprises elements of all three—honor, face, and dignity—cultures. According to Friedrichs, status anxiety affects different cultures to various degrees, but in general "concerns with status and humiliation mediate the social and political effects of honor, face, and dignity culture" (Friedrichs 2016: 64).

The concepts of self-worth, self-esteem, self-respect and self-regard have many common features. But in the context of relationship between diplomatic Self and Other, we prefer to employ "self-regard" as a positive sense of self that emerges from relations of Others to the Self. In diplomacy, self-regard is an essential element of the efficiency of the diplomatic actor's interactions with other actors. Self-regard drives diplomatic actors to seek social status, and social status feeds self-regard. Any threat to the diplomatic actor's self-regard is a threat to its Selfness. Diplomatic culture tries to protect the diplomatic actors from lowering their self-regard—otherwise no diplomacy may happen.

In modern international relations theory, the threat to sense of Self is theorized in relationship to the concept of ontological security. This concept, developed in sociology by Anthony Giddens (1991), is reflected in understanding international relations and politics (Mitzen 2006; Steele 2008; Rumelili 2015). States, in addition to physical security, "also seek ontological security, or security of the self" (Mitzen 2006: 341). They pursue ontological security for maintaining consistent self-concepts, and they carry on social actions to serve their self-identity needs even when these actions threaten their physical existence (Steele 2008). Self is always a socially developed Self, and self-concept, self-knowledge, self-consciousness, self-awareness, self-image, or, in general, sense of Self, expresses the Self's perception of itself in a social context, in relations to Other(s).

Studying the threat to Self, namely to its ontological security, Janice Bially Mattern pointed to "identity violence" (2007: 7). Self, according to Bially Mattern, is constructed sociolinguistically, i.e. socially through discourse. Therefore, it may be threatened by "a nonphysical but nevertheless coercive form of power that is exercised through language" (Bially Mattern 2005, 583). She defines such power as the "representational force". This forceful threat uses linguistic means and is derived "from inconsistencies and contradictions in the victim's Self" (Bially Mattern 2005: 603). In other words, Self, constituted sociolinguistically, is vulnerable to the fragility of its sociolinguistic "realities" (Bially Mattern 2005: 586). Representational force, according to Bially Mattern, appears not as a direct violent attack but as identity violence. So this approach points to the links between language (which is a symbolic system), the sociolinguistically constructed Self, and identity violence.

Philippe Braud (2014) analyzed "symbolic violence", not in the pure Bourdieuian tradition, but in relations to self-representation and identity, and his approach also fits into the study of ontological security. According to Braud, the criterion of any violence is the suffering experiences by a victim, and in the case of symbolic violence, damage operates at the level of self-representation. Braud stressed an important element that is relevant to our research: symbolic violence affects identity, and it aims at lowering or even destroying the self-esteem of an individual or a collective. Braud also pointed to a specific relationship between international diplomacy and symbolic violence: according to him, the codified language and etiquette of diplomacy can be explained by a concern for avoiding a terminology and behavior that can be perceived as symbolically violent by the adversary. Although Braud did not offer a more detailed explanation of this important point about diplomacy, his ideas are valuable for the development of our arguments.

Diplomacy exists "only in the scene of the other" (Constantinou 1996: 117). It is a highly elaborated channel of national Selves encounters. A positive sense of Self is not a luxury but a necessary condition for the diplomatic actor's integrity, confidence, reputation and effectiveness in interactions with Other. For the actor, Self is manifested in its sense of Self. No Self exists without sense of Self, and the actor's ability to sense—perceive and feel—its Self acquires a great significance for maintaining and protecting the Selfness, inner integrity. Therefore, symbolic insult hurting diplomatic actor's sense of Self emerges as a matter of ontological security. Sensuality, feelings and emotions appear as vital areas of ontological security as a security of Self.

Both insult and humiliation (because of insulting behavior) are emotional behaviors. Even when performed with cold calculation, an insult is affected by emotions. The humiliated side can also try to control itself and not show emotions; nonetheless, humiliation is a deeply emotional and affective state. For good reason, the U.S. Department of State put "composure"—"to stay calm, poised, and effective in stressful or difficult situations; to think on one's feet, adjusting quickly to changing situations; to maintain self-control" as one of basic qualifications of a foreign service officer (2017).

Todd Hall (2015) studied a state level official display of emotional behavior toward other states—emotional diplomacy, as he called it. According to Hall, emotional diplomacy represents the intentional and coordinated effort of state officials and policy makers to project the image of particular emotions of the state. But individuals who participate in this coordinated effort may not necessarily experience the official—state level emotions. Analyzing diplomacy of anger, diplomacy of sympathy and diplomacy of guilt as manifestations of diplomacy of emotion, Hall pointed to the strategic character of such emotional displays. In other words, for the state actor, emotional diplomacy is a strategic performance which is employed "to prevent further violations of their interests, to seek to refashion their relations with other states, and to rehabilitate their image on the international stage" (Hall 2015: 187). Hall, using Erving Goffman's dramaturgical model, connected emotional diplomacy with the interactional impression management performance.

Symbolic insult in diplomacy, as we will see further on, is a manipulative act. The insulters—both at state and personal levels—can try to hide their emotions while insulting, or make a false emotional impression. Insult in diplomacy can also be committed by demonstrating a certain official state level emotions of the actor when the Other may expect a different emotional reaction. In other words, Self can be insulted from a difference between the expected and expressed emotional reaction from Other. For example, the absence of condolences[15] from a significant Other to the death of a country's leader, or

15 Diplomatic condolences as any other meaningful messages in diplomacy can be a very interesting area of political, social, cultural, linguistic and psychological studies. Ben Fenton-Smith (2007) analyzed the social function of international discourse in relation with the expression of diplomatic condolences. By focusing "on the discursive strategies of world leaders in the wake of Yasser Arafat's death", this study "demonstrates how global political leaders compose their versions of a world order and position themselves within it" (Fenton-Smith 2007: 697). Condolences express sympathy, but they may contain the risk of insult if compiled clumsily or expressed with inappropriate body language. In diplomacy, both the content and tone of the message play a significant role.

sympathy in connection to a natural disaster can be perceived as an insulting behavior. Therefore, adequate and accurate expression of an emotional reaction of Self to some event related to Other has a great importance in diplomacy.

Insult in diplomacy can emerge as a calculated strategic action or as an emotional reaction to an assault. Often negative emotions beget negative emotions. As Wendt pointed out, "Negative self-images tend to emerge from perceived disregard or humiliation by other states, and as such may occur frequently in highly competitive international environments (the Germans after World War I? the Russians today?). Since groups cannot long tolerate such images if they are to meet the self-esteem needs of their members, they will compensate by self-assertion and/or devaluation and aggression toward the Other" (Wendt 1999: 236–237). Diplomatic symbolic insult can represent one of the ways of such a reaction. Thus, the diplomatic actors' sense of place, self-regard, ontological security and emotional state are locked into one chain.

There are various levels and intensities of experiencing the Self, sense of Self and threat to Self. Diplomacy is a specific fine art with its face-management, "tiny" moves and peculiar delicate perception of the world. Not everything is visible in a political and social game of diplomacy. It is an art where sensitivity and assertiveness, tact and firmness, openness and secrecy get along. Sometimes diplomats from unfriendly countries can smile to each other and make nice handshakes but at the same time experience some threat to their sense of collective Self. The mind of a diplomat who host a diplomatic reception can be involved in analyzing things like who did not come, why he or she didn't attend, what does that mean, etc. These questions might be quite silly for many outsiders who may think differently about diplomatic profession, but they affect diplomats' sense of Self. So, from diplomacy's perspective, even small diplomatic incidents, embarrassments and insults appear as meaningful occurrences. Diplomats, because of the character of their profession, try to catch even the slightest threat to the ontological security of their country. The part of diplomatic sense of reality is realizing that any diplomatic insult, even a mild one, have an escalatory potential in a deteriorated political environment.

Three Types of Insult in Diplomacy

There is a clear symbolic dimension of physical violence against a country's significant architectural sights, historical monuments and other visible substances including diplomatic missions abroad or ambassadors. Diplomacy, because of its representational nature, is saturated with symbolism. Diplomats officially represent their countries internationally, so their existence and interactions have clear symbolic dimension. That is why diplomatic actors' Selves—which are very sensitive to the matters of recognition and honor, as we already discussed—are vulnerable to symbolic insult. Therefore, in diplomacy, disgracing diplomats, or injuring their self-regard and social status as well as mistreating national symbols are likely to be perceived as symbolic insult. Improper symbolism, for example, the abuse of a national flag or emblem as well as the disgracing of an individual diplomat, threatens and hurts the diplomatic actor's sense of Self. When one actor deliberately manipulates with self-related, i.e. ontologically significant symbols in order to downgrade the opponent's self-regard and social status, the latter may become a victim of humiliation.

An example of a symbolic insult took place at the presidential level in June 2017 when Ukraine was granted visa-free travel to the European Union. "President Petro Poroshenko hailed it as a 'final break' with the 'Russian Empire,' quoting 19th-century Russian poet Mikhail Lermontov with a smile: 'Farewell, unwashed Russia!'" Within a few days, Russian President Vladimir Putin fired back at Poroshenko, "quoting the poem in its entirety, Putin used it to suggest that Ukraine is historically a province of Russia and to quip that Ukraine should have its guard up in 'gay' Europe" (Balmforth 2017). Putin also "advised Ukraine's leadership to close their offshore bank accounts at first before becoming Europeans" (TASS Russian News Agency 2017 a). In the context of Russian-Ukrainian conflict over Crimea and Eastern Ukraine, Mikhail Lermontov's name, one of the highly regarded symbols of Russian poetry, was in the center of a quarrel between the highest representatives of the two countries. In other words, the two presidents tried to use Lermontov's name and poetry as a means of symbolic insult.

Symbolic insult can be linked to both material and ideational factors. Material objects and culture play a prominent role in diplomacy (Rudolph and Metzig 2016), and diplomatic actors need to be sensitive to both their worth and meaning. Based on media reports, Harriet Rudolph provided some examples of diplomatic confusions related to material culture: in 2009, the removal of a bust of Winston Churchill from the White House caused tensions between the United Kingdom and the United States. In 2011, the imbalance of gift exchange happened between the President of France Nicolas Sarkozy and President of the United States Barack Obama: the French side's gift included fine crystal, a golf bag, table lamps on silver pedestals, and a sculpture of Alexander the Great's horse, a total worth more than $41,000, but the American side's gift was a collection of DVDs. In 2015, President of Iran Hassan Rohani refused to take part in a state dinner in Paris because the menu included wine, and "He even rejected the compromise that French authorities quickly offered to smooth intercultural tension: a "petit-déjeuner" served without alcoholic drinks. In Rohani's opinion, any kind of meal described as "petit" would be unable to adequately reflect either his position as head of state or the prestige of his country" (2016: 5). Obviously, the symbolism behind the material objects plays a significant role in their assessment and role in diplomacy.

In diplomacy, the matters of social status such as primacy, equality, honor and respect play an even more significant role in diplomatic actors' self-regard and relationship arrangements. Modern diplomacy, obviously, doesn't practice physical insult, although in the past, ambassadors could engage in dueling because of disputes over the precedence. Harold Nicolson provided some interesting cases of such a struggle for primacy in diplomatic history:

> In the old days the Pope claimed the right to decide in what order the nations of the world should be listed, and there exists a memorandum of 1504 in which this order is laid down. The Pope, not unnaturally, placed himself first among the monarchs of the earth. The Emperor came second and after him his heir-apparent, "The King of the Romans." Then followed the Kings of France, Spain, Aragon and Portugal. Great Britain came sixth on the list and the King of Denmark last. This papal class-list was not accepted without demur by the sovereigns concerned. It often happened that a French Ambassador had been instructed by his sovereign in no case to yield precedence to the Spanish Ambassador, whereas the latter had received exactly similar instructions. Undignified scenes took place at court functions; at a court ball in London in 1768, a scuffle took place between the French and Russian Ambassadors which terminated in a duel.
>
> A classic example of these struggles for precedence is the case of the Spanish Ambassador's carriage in 1661. It was in those days the custom for foreign envoys to make their entry with a great apparatus of state. Their foreign colleagues were expected to send their gala coaches in order to add magnificence to the procession. Thus when, on September 30, 1661, a new Swedish envoy disembarked at the Tower wharf in London, both the Spanish and the French Ambassadors had sent their coaches to greet him. The Swedish envoy sanded, entered the royal coach which had been lent to meet him, and drove off. The French Ambassador's coachman edged his horses immediately behind the Swedish equipage, an action which was regarded by the coachman of the Spanish Ambassador as a direct insult to the King of Spain.
>
> A struggle ensued which (since each coach had been accompanied by some 150 armed men) assumed serious proportions. The French

> coachman was pulled from his box, two of the horses were hamstrung, and a postilion was killed. Louis XIV thereupon severed diplomatic relations with Spain, and threatened to declare war unless a full apology were given and the Spanish Ambassador in London were punished. The King of Spain, anxious to avoid hostilities, agreed to make the necessary apologies and reparation.
>
> NICOLSON 1939: 179–180

The symbolic game of precedence could include the order on the list and in the entrance, place of coaches in the procession, the seating plan around a dinner or a conference table, the sequence of putting signatures under agreements and so on. "Today we often speak of 'national prestige' or 'national honour': these important factors of power were, in the earlier centuries, symbolized by the order of precedence. It represented to them something analogous to what 'insults to the flag' represented to later generations" (Nicolson 1939: 182). So, in diplomacy, the actor's prestige and honor symbolically expressed in order of precedence, can be threatened by the violation of the accepted symbolic order.

Nowadays, the obscure forms of symbolic insult in diplomacy are often observed and reported on by journalists. Paul Reynolds, in his BBC news post entitled "Snub—part of the diplomatic game", noted that "the snub is an accepted part of the delicate diplomatic life, and done deftly, can make a point", and "they are often signs of an underlying problem" (2010). Media journalism often refers to "diplomatic snub", "symbolic snub" in diplomacy, "diplomatic slap" and "diplomatic slap in the face". In diplomacy, cutting diplomatic ties, recalling ambassadors, refusing meetings and declining invitations are usually considered as snubs. Diplomacy may use even more sophisticated, understated and manipulative practices of "slapping in the face", while pretending that nothing happened. Such manipulative practices of elusive insult and humiliation can also be built on the subtle use of diplomatic symbolism.

Diplomats have always been associated with high social status, and diplomacy has always been linked with glorious ceremonies and symbolic honoring of states. In addition, international legal norms support the equality of states. But the act of insulting is asserting dominance, "either intentionally claiming superiority or unintentionally revealing lack of regard", and being insulted "is to suffer a shock, a disruption of one's sense of self and one's place in the world" (Neu 2008: vii). Therefore, the very presence of insults is contrary to the spirit of diplomacy. "To accept an insult is to submit, in certain worlds to be dishonored" (Neu 2008: vii), and no nations want to be disgraced in diplomatic arena where status and honor represent such values. However, diplomacy is a part of international politics and it may use symbolic insult for political purposes in specific ways.

We distinguish three major forms of insult in diplomacy: (1) non-recognition, or ignorance, or neglect, or indifference—figuratively, such alienating behavior can be called *diplomatic bypassing*, (2) direct—verbal or nonverbal—offence, that we metaphorically call the *diplomatic punch*, and (3) indirect, or tacit debasement that can allegorically be called the *diplomatic slap*. These varieties of insult can take place in a more or less pure or mixed forms. Although diplomatic bypassing, punching and slapping may employ different behavioral patterns, they also contain substantial symbolism.

As Thomas Conley remarked, one individual's or group's insults against another individual or group can result in different reactions—a punch in the face, duel in some societies, riot, diplomatic crisis, or even war, "so the matter of 'intensity,' of a scale of 'hurt,' comes into consideration—in both sanctioned and unsanctioned insults" (2010: 4). Apparently, the matter of intensity or hurt affects the reaction to the insult. However, considering international diplomacy as a social and political game with its cultural and legal, open and hidden norms and rules, we can also consider the "gamesmanship" aspect of diplomatic insults and reactions to them. As a part of the symbolic game of international diplomacy, "bypassing", "punching" and "slapping" can provoke various exposed or concealed reactions which would depend on different political, moral, social and legal factors and their relations. Sometimes, non-reaction can be a more powerful diplomatic instrument than immediate reaction. This is the area of diplomatic strategic gamesmanship.

Diplomatic Bypassing

Recognition is a fundamental factor for the diplomatic actor's Self. In fact, recognition appears as the existential and legal act for a diplomatic actor: diplomatic relations can be established only on the basis of mutual recognition. As Charles Taylor pointed out, recognition is a vital human need that has a link with identity, and "our identity is partly shaped by recognition or its absence, often by the *mis*recognition of others, and so a person or group of people can suffer real damage, real distortion, if the people or society around them mirror back to them a confining or demeaning or contemptible picture of themselves" (1994: 25). People encounter one another with expectations for recognition, and the denial of recognition may lead to the diminishing of self-respect, humiliation and degradation (Honneth 1996: 164–165). Hannes Kuch pointed to the symbolic dimension of violations of human dignity, "rituality" of humiliation that has its roots in the symbolic dimension of recognition (2011). Dignity appears as "a particular form of vulnerability—a symbolic vulnerability", and "not only acts of recognition but also acts of misrecognition, and of humiliation, have a constitutive symbolic dimension" (Kuch 2011: 37). The same applies to acts of respect and disrespect (Kuch 2011: 50).

By playing a game of recognition and misrecognition, international diplomacy can contribute to a sense of national pride or disgrace. In diplomacy, the main motive of misrecognition appears to be political. However, in general, misrecognition can be nuanced and also caused by a psychological reason of ambivalence. A group may know that another deserves its recognition, but, since granting such recognition would disadvantage that group, it fails to do so (Thompson and Hoggett 2016). As a tool of foreign policy, diplomacy can be influenced by the public mood as well as the moods of individual political decision makers. For example, as Nora Femenia (2000) explored, in the Falklands/Malvinas crisis, emotional factors, specifically, national self-images, were the central motivations behind the decisions made by both Britain and Argentina.

Diplomacy can practice various forms of misrecognition. Apart from open denial of diplomatic recognition, actors may exercise more elusive forms of bypassing each other such as lowering the level or intensity of communication, disregarding accomplishments, overlooking intentions, neglecting historical facts or events, "forgetting" to respond for a letter or appreciate favors, abandoning promises, refusing to meet or invite, rejecting invitations, waiting in the hallway, ignoring national holidays, etc. All forms of such a bypassing may severely affect the diplomatic actors' sense of Selves, threaten their integrity, social being and ontological existence.

Diplomatic Punch

Diplomatic actors can enter direct confrontational verbal wrangles, use abusive metaphorical language, threaten, or employ nonverbal offensive actions such as moving troops to the mutual border, or exploit other hostile means like boycotts, expulsion of diplomats, violation of diplomatic immunities, political and economic sanctions, or suspension from a respected international organization. From a diplomatic perspective, these types of nasty moves have clear symbolic significance and directed meaning.[16] Barry O'Neil, for example, studied insult as assault on face that led to war (2002: 139–163). "Insults from

16 Even unintentional insults in international politics may have symbolic dimensions. For example, in May 7, 1999, during the Kosovo war the U.S. Air Force accidental bombing destroyed the Embassy of People's Republic of China in Belgrade, Federal Republic of Yugoslavia and killed several people. That was seen by China as a major international insult—"barbaric attack" (BBC 1999 b). The U.S. apology as a symbolic act was a part of the settlement (on apologies in U.S.-China diplomacy: Cornut 2011).

diplomats may be rare, but they seem to have been more common as preludes to a war" (O'Neil 2002: 139). As he remarked, many diplomatic insults were more than careless phrases which provoked an emotional response—they had a strategic point and a connection to violence.

One of the harshest diplomatic symbolic insult is the murder of a diplomat. As Noé Cornago puts it, "the singular symbolism that the dead body of the diplomat, perhaps even more than the living one, invariably entails" (2015: 1). We can also consider the stigma and stigmatization in international relations (Adler-Nissen 2014) as a form of pungent insult that may have direct impact on the diplomatic actors' behavior and relationships. Adverse international relations, for example between the U.S. and Iran, or the U.S. and North Korea, or between Israel and Iran, or between Israel and some Arab countries contribute to the use of symbolic insult by diplomatic representatives of the adversary states.

States, as diplomatic actors, rarely use direct threats. Diplomats typically use "understated ways of referring to the use of force—war" by referring to "all means necessary" or "face serious consequences" (Langhotz 2004: 15). But sometimes countries openly threaten others like North Korea' nuclear threat to the American territory Guam (Lendon and Berlinger 2017). This verbal threat came after North Korea's launch of a missile over Japan on August 29, 2017. But as any message, direct and indirect threats need to be understood in historical and current political and cultural settings. In a wider sense, a threat can be an element of a bargaining strategy. Some politicians and observers see the North Korean missile launches as a serious threat but others perceive them mostly as a provocation or bravado, or even a predominantly symbolic act. As a reaction to North Korea's missile shot over Japan, the United States President Donald Trump said that "all options are on the table" (Berlinger and Wakatsuki 2017), but earlier he also warned North Korea by saying that "They will be met with fire and fury like the world has never seen" (Thrush and Bakeraug 2017).[17] So, international actors need to appropriately read and send messages, and understand the symbolism behind them.

Coercive diplomacy—with its threat to use force or a combination of using soft diplomatic instruments with the actual use of force—can also attract symbolic insult to influence the opponent and abuse its sense of Self. But this paper mostly focuses on practices of "soft", "invisible", "obscure", "intangible",

17 During the following weeks, mutual accusations and threats continued and even escalated.

"elusive", "tacit" and essentially ambivalent and manipulative forms of symbolic insult in diplomacy that usually do not lead to war or the break of diplomatic relations.

Opposing countries can blame each other for various things, for example, condemn the other side's human rights records or accuse them of wrongdoing and making harm. But apart from open assaults, countries can use some bizarre and intricate ways of offending. For instance, in the midst of the Cold War, a type of confrontation occurred between Cuba and some Western countries headed by the USA. On the Feast of the Epiphany, diplomats from the Spanish embassy dressed as the Three Kings and went in horse-drawn carriages through Old Havana throwing out sweets for children, and "the Cuban authorities accused them of deliberately setting up a scene in which hungry, desperate Cuban children would have to scrabble in the gutters" (The Economist 2001).

Diplomatic actors and the public are quite sensitive to ambiguous offences which tend to use symbolic means. On the one hand, they may ignore such insults because they are not obvious. But on the other hand, most observers recognize the hidden, symbolic meaning of unstated insults. Apart from humiliating the opponent and making the Self fragile, symbolic insult in diplomacy may negatively affect relationships between states and other international actors, and may cause strong retaliation from the victim's side.

Diplomatic Slap

This topic—how diplomatic actors use symbolic abuses indirectly, ambivalently and covertly in their customary intercourse as a means of manipulative influence, maneuvers and bargaining by ontologically threatening their opponents' sense of Self—has not yet received much attention from international relations and diplomatic scholars. The significance of the diplomatic actor's self-regard makes using symbolic insult in international politics and diplomacy peculiar. Diplomacy is a delicate activity where the matters of identity, dignity, pride, honor, respect and social status play a significant role, and that is why even a "small" but symbolically annoying action of one actor upon the self-regard of the other actor could be considered by the latter as an insult or a humiliating act, although the offender may ignore such a disgraceful action. Since diplomacy employs highly normative and relational practices, any symbolically significant abuse of protocol or other social norms and cultural patterns can also be seen by diplomatic actors and public as an act of offence or insult.

Because of the importance and the widespread use of symbolism in international diplomacy by both powerful and weak actors, they can employ concealed forms of offence against each other or the equal. Tacit humiliation allows, on the one hand, to make a point and "lower" an opponent, and on the other, to keep the relationship "as usual". In other words, that is quite a "diplomatic" way of confronting and degrading an adversary. Symbolic insult can also be a self-affirmative action: through humiliating an opponent, diplomatic actors may try to protect or uplift their sense of Selves.

A slap, even a physical one, "is generally regarded as a symbolic gesture rather than a serious physical assault" (Neu 2008: 148), and "the injury in a slap is generally more symbolic than physical" (Neu 2008: 41). This is especially true in the diplomatic sphere, where a significant part of interactions takes place at a symbolic level and through symbolic means. Slap as a symbolic gesture is not supposed to break the relationship between those who slapped and who was slapped. Slap appears as a certain aggression but its "softness" and mainly symbolic nature usually allow the insulter and insulted to keep some relationship. As a symbolic phenomenon, a diplomatic slap emerges as a game of meanings: symbols express meaning, and both the insulter and insulted are engaged in operations with meanings. So, the diplomatic slap or snub represents a meaningful act: it makes a point. However, in contrast to the obvious strike or "diplomatic punch", the diplomatic slap needs to be an ambiguous act. Such a multi-semantic behavior also needs to be properly delivered and interpreted.

Diplomatic slap may have serious consequences when it happens in a politically explosive situation. On July 13, 1870, Prussian Chancellor Otto von Bismarck edited and then released a telegram he received from King of Prussia William I (the Ems telegram): Bismarck did so to provoke France to war with Prussia. There were fundamental political, geopolitical and ontological causes of the Franco-Prussian War (1870–1871), but the original telegram and the edited one were seen by some key figures in Germany and France as "slap in the face" and detonated the war.[18]

---

18 The Ems dispatch was related to the events around the Prussian candidacy of Leopold, Prince of Hohenzollern, to the Spanish throne. France opposed Leopold's candidacy, and Prince of Hohenzollern's candidacy was withdrawn. Nevertheless, France—through its Ambassador to the court of Prussia Count Vincent Benedetti—demanded from the Prussian King in Bad Ems a formal assurance that no member of the Hohenzollern family would pretend to the Spanish throne. "The king politely refused Benedetti's demand, and their discussion ended", but "Bismarck's edited version, which he published the next day, omitted the courtesies in the two men's exchange and instead made it seem that each man had insulted the other" (Encyclopædia Britannica 2014).

The conversation between the King and the Ambassador was carefully edited by Bismarck. "Whereas the original dispatch spoke of Wilhelm putting off the audience with Benedetti because confirmation had been received of Prince Leopold's withdrawal, Bismarck's rewritten version had the king gruffly canceling the audience without

Sometimes even "innocent" rhetoric acts—jokes and irony may comprise insult (Colney 2010: 28). Some jokes may not be funny but insulting (Neu 2008: 22). "Joke's hidden purpose" (Neu 2008: 220) or meaning needs to be interpreted, and in diplomacy, sometimes, publicly explained. Occasionally statesmen, government officials, diplomats or other international players may use jokes in their communication, or tease one another, and eventually—especially if it happens publicly—that can carry a risk of embarrassment or humiliation. For example, on March 24, 2016, President of Russia Vladimir Putin met the United States Secretary of State John Kerry in the Kremlin. At the beginning of this meeting, the Russian president "teased Secretary of State John Kerry, who was visiting in Moscow, for carrying his own luggage, asking whether it was a sign that the U.S. is somehow struggling" (Toosi 2016). When the subject of the teasing is the head of a foreign ministry or a whole country, there is a possibility of, to put it mildly, a misunderstanding. Some observers can see this as a symbolic offence with a humiliating potential. Through his or her reaction to the ambiguous joke, the diplomat can smooth out or aggravate the situation. Kerry "took Putin's ribbing in stride", and replied: "When we have a private moment, I'll show you what's in my briefcase", and "I think you'll be surprised—pleasantly" (Toosi 2016). Apparently, public perception of this kind of exchange depends on both their content and context, including the state of bilateral relations, wider international situation, cultural norms, interlocutors' ranks, personal

---

explanation" (Wawro 2003: 37). As Geoffrey Wawro pointed out, "Bismarck had deliberately fanned war fever in July 1870 to generate popular support for national unification. The Ems telegram had been a brilliant piece of theater that had converted a dynastic insult into a national one, and Bismarck (and his loyal newspaper editors) had billed the looming conflict as "a great national war" against "foreign aggression and presence" on sacred German soil" (Wawro 2003: 301).

In his memoirs Bismarck (1898), commenting on his edit of the Ems telegram, had referred to the "honour", "Spanish sense of honour", "extorted submission a humiliation of Germany for which I did not desire to be responsible", "wound to our sense of national honour", "humiliation before France", "to protect national honour and independence", "our national sense of honour", "honour of Prussia and of the national confidence in it", and "a question of national honour" which, according to the Prussian Chancellor, prompted him to edit the King's dispatch and incite the war with France. Bismarck thought that the edited telegram "will have the effect of a red rag upon the Gallic bull" (1898: 101). After reading the King's telegram and conversing with the Minister of War, von Roon, Bismarck remarked that "we had got our slap in the face from France" (1898: 95). The same feeling experienced the French foreign minister Duc de Gramont upon reading the edited Ems telegram: he felt himself as "a man who has just been slapped in the face" (Wetzel 2001: 165).

relationship, body language, place of interaction, etc. Furthermore, diplomatic skill is a crucial factor that can help the parties to get out of an awkward situation with dignity.

A slap can be accidental or deliberative, "but it is the intention behind the deliberate one (at least in certain social situations) that turns it into an insult" (Neu 2008: 12). Diplomats may use tacit but calculated insult to humiliate the opponent to a certain extent. Total humiliation of the opponent goes beyond the social game of diplomacy. Sometimes it is even difficult to detect elusive diplomatic slaps by revealing its intention.

For example, an intimidating episode took place during a visit of the German Chancellor Angela Merkel to the Russian President Vladimir Putin's summer residence in Sochi where the host brought out his large black Labrador Koni (Le Miere 2017). "While that might be a treat for many guests, it was not so pleasant for Merkel, who has had a fear of dogs since being bitten by one in 1995. The accompanying image of Putin sitting back and smirking as Merkel tensed up in anxiety spoke volumes" (Le Miere 2017). Although Putin later denied he knew about Merkel's fear, the German Chancellor said that she "understand why he has to do this—to prove he's a man" (Le Miere 2017). These were some news headlines about that episode: "That time Putin brought his dog to a meeting to scare Angela Merkel" (2017); "Vladimir Putin denies setting his dog on Angela Merkel" (Oliphant 2016). These kinds of ambiguous situations can raise various interpretations since they are affected by the experiences and attitudes of the interpreters.

International situation, political interests and historical memory can greatly affect the interpretation of symbolism and symbolic behavior. Certain behavior in a symbolically sensitive setting may cause political tensions and deteriorate diplomatic relations. Analyzing conflicts between Japan and its neighbors namely China and South Korea over Yasukuni Shrine visits by Japanese politicians, M. Erika Pollmann refers to "symbolic provocative behaviors" (2016: 133). Yasukuni shrine, built in Tokyo in 1869, is the burial place of about 2.5 million people who died for Japan, 1068 of whom are convicted war criminals, including 14 Class-A war criminals. So, this Shinto shrine has a controversial but a very negative symbolism for China and South Korea.

In a modern history, every time when Japanese politicians visited Yasukuni shrine, this outraged China and South Korea and caused their strong protests. Former Japanese Prime Minister Junichiro Koizumi visited the shrine 5 times, and although he explained his visits as private, they generated a fierce response from abroad. Current Prime Minister of Japan Shinzo Abe visited the shrine once in 2013. He said that it was "an anti-war gesture", but "China called the visit 'absolutely unacceptable to the Chinese people', and Seoul expressed 'regret and anger'" (BBC News 2013). As Rupert Wingfield-Hayes pointed out, "Whatever Shinzo Abe says, any visit to the Yasakuni shrine by a Japanese prime minister is deeply political and sure to cause offence" (BBC News 2013). The following two headlines eloquently describe the whole picture: "Yasukuni shrine visits: Japan honoring the dead or insulting the neighbors?" (Park 2013), and "A slap in the face" (The Economist 2014).

For the Japanese politicians visiting the shrine has both domestic and international applications: undertaking this action, they consider the cost of each (Pollmann 2016). For the countries affected, such visits also have another dyadic dimension which expresses the collusion of their international political and relationship aspirations. Due to certain internal and external factors, international political or relational motives and expected benefits can prevail. As Pollmann pointed out, Japanese politicians' visit the Yasukuni shrine—whether they take place or not—become an important issue in Northeast Asia's regional diplomacy, and the conflict over this shrine "reflects a broader trend in the region: using WWII remembrance as a political tool" (2016: 150). All this demonstrate that the power and interpretational properties of symbolic actions and interactions in international politics and diplomacy are affected by the variety of internal and external, political, historical, moral, emotional, relational and other factors.

Symbolism, Diplomatic Humiliation and Embarrassment

Humiliation is the other side of an insult, or, to say differently, a negative emotional reaction of the victim or observer exposed to an abuse. As a social act, humiliation occurs in discrepant interaction between Self and Other. The act of deliberately insulting means the actor is counting on humiliating the other. Humiliation is "about putting down and holding down" (Lindner 2006: 3), and "to humiliate someone is to assert power over him by denying and destroying his status claims" (Burton 2014). It is an emotion that lowers someone's self-worth, self-respect and dignity by stripping away and revealing as false and illegitimate affectations (Saurette 2006: 507–509). In diplomatic history, there have been cases which could be viewed as a severe symbolic humiliation of one actor by the other, or as an attempt to humiliate. We can refer to such well-known cases as the humiliation of Holy Roman Emperor Henry IV by Pope Gregory VII when in January 1077 the latter made the former wait outside in the cold weather in northern Italy for three days before granting him the revocation of his excommunication (Hamm 2010: 177; Maxwell 2010: 77). Another example is the relinquishment of the British envoy William Pitt Amherst's mission to China in 1816 because of his refusal to perform the *kowtow*—kneeling and deep bowing before the Chinese emperor (Encyclopedia Britannica 1998).[19]

Hans Morgenthau provided an example of a diplomatic practice of self-affirmation through the humiliation of others. At the end of the eighteenth century, foreign ambassadors who presented themselves to the Sultan of Constantinople, "were grabbed by the arms by court officials and their heads bent down", and after the customary exchange of speeches between the ambassador and the representative of the Sultan, the court officials exclaimed: "Praise be to the Eternal that the infidels must come and give homage to our gloriously brilliant scepter" (1993: 87). As Morgenthau pointed out, "the humiliation of the representatives of foreign countries was intended to symbolize the inferiority in power of the countries they represented" (1993: 87). However, judging historical humiliations is difficult because humiliation is the Self's social feeling, and what seems to some as extremely humiliating, might have been a different experience for another in the other historical and social contexts.

Humiliation has a long history of causing violence but it became an important subject of geopolitical scrutiny and public awareness in the modern world (Hartling, Lindner, Spalthoff, and Britton 2013: 64). Humiliation "is a powerful derogatory force" that can "awaken a desire and a movement to remove its stigma, and to remove with the causes of humiliation" (Mazlish and Weisbrode 2014). But an intangible humiliation in diplomacy appears as manipulative practice that may allow the offender to disgrace the other side and at the same time try to continue "business as usual". So, diplomats may practice symbolic insult with hope that the other side would "swallow" it even though being humiliated. However, because of the emotional nature of humiliation, the victim can react in a very acute form. Here is Aaron Klein's (2010) account of a diplomatic incident which he described as a well-planned symbolic humiliation of a diplomat.

> The fire was set on the evening of Jan. 11, when Israel's Deputy Foreign Minister, Danny Ayalon, summoned Turkey's ambassador Ahmet Oguz Celikkol to an urgent meeting. Its purpose was to deliver Israel's

19 In 1793 the first British envoy to China George Macartney refused to kneel with both knees on the ground during the meeting with the Chinese emperor even though the Chinese side insisted on this ceremony. Finally, both parties agreed that Macartney would perform kneeling down on one knee as he usually did to his own king (Robbins 2010: 304).

> complaints about a Turkish TV series that portrays Israeli soldiers as baby killers. At the meeting, Ayalon was caught on camera instructing the Israeli TV news crew covering the event to make sure that its footage captured the fact that Celikkol had been deliberately seated on a chair lower than that of his Israeli counterpart, that only the Israeli flag was on the table (without the Turkish one, as would be the norm at a diplomatic photo op) and that Ayalon and his colleagues are not smiling at the ambassador. The symbolic humiliation of the Turkish diplomat was a well-planned if clumsy expression of the new policy of Ayalon and his boss, hard-line Foreign Minister Avigdor Lieberman, who have decried what they see as the tendency of Israeli diplomats to ingratiate themselves with foreign interlocutors. The offending Turkish TV program, Ayalon seemed to believe, was not a moment for diplomatic niceties; national pride demanded a retaliatory humiliation of the Turks.

The symbolism of this interaction with the absence of one flag and the difference in the arrangement of the chairs clearly points to a diplomatic snub. "One Israeli newspaper marked the height difference on the photo, and captioned it 'the height of humiliation'" (Head 2010). This incident "was taken as an intolerable national insult in Turkey" (Klein 2010), and "Ankara demanded an apology for what it described as Ayalon's demeaning treatment of its ambassador" (Ravid 2010). In other words, Turkey's collective sense of Self was hurt.

Ayalon's initial apology was rejected by the Turkish side, but then the Israeli side offered a formal apology which was accepted by Ankara. Commenting on this incident, the then President of Israel, Shimon Peres, said that Ayalon's treatment of the Turkish ambassador "was not diplomatic" and "reflected the 'mistake of one man, not of the state'" (Ravid 2010). Calming down a diplomatic incident is a part of diplomatic practice of keeping relations between Self and Other.

Insult, when performed publicly and seen as extremely destructive, can leave little chances for maintaining relationships between the sides, although sometimes, diplomacy can try to save relations by "sweetening the pill". To say it differently, "selling" or "appropriately" presenting for the domestic audience or the opponent the harsh move in foreign policy and diplomacy can be a part of the diplomatic game of insult. That kind of game happened when the United States was insulted by the Russian meddling in the 2016 U.S. election (Russia has denied any involvement), and Russia, for its part, was insulted by the new sanctions imposed on it from the American side. In July 2017, the United States House of Representatives and Senate voted overwhelmingly to impose new sanctions on Russia, Iran and North Korea. Russian President

Vladimir Putin "has accused US lawmakers of 'insolence', and promised Russia will retaliate if the latest round of US sanctions against Russia are signed into law" (Walker 2017). In such a tense situation, on July 29, 2017, the U.S. Secretary of State Rex W. Tillerson issued the following press statement on this sanctions legislation: "The near unanimous votes for the sanctions legislation in Congress represent the strong will of the American people to see Russia take steps to improve relations with the United States. We hope that there will be cooperation between our two countries on major global issues and these sanctions will no longer be necessary. We will work closely with our friends and Allies to ensure our messages to Russia, Iran, and North Korea are clearly understood" (Tillerson 2017).

Since the Trump administration didn't want these new sanctions on Russia but the U.S. Congress overwhelmingly supported them, this press statement can be seen as a kind of diplomatic neutralization of the insult on Russia in order to keep some working relationship between the parties. But in relations with such a public slap in the face, Russian officials tried to mock the statement. "Russia derides Tillerson statement on sanction", was a headline of an AP article in the Washington Post (Lee 2017). Here is what this article said: "With respect to Russia, at least, the message did not appear to be understood, as the Russian Embassy in Washington said in a series of tweets that it was bewildered. 'The statement made by the @StateDept on July 29 regarding a new sanctions legislation approved by Congress cannot but raise eyebrows,' it said. 'Washington still doesn't get the fact that pressure never works against @Russia, bilateral relations can hardly be improved by sanctions'" (Lee 2017). Within a few days after his press statement, Tillerson admitted that America's relationship with Russia was at an all-time low and deteriorating (Mindock 2017).

Dishonor destroys the spirit of diplomacy, and disregard is an undiplomatic action by nature. Both receiving and providing honor are meaningful acts in diplomacy, aspects of diplomatic social practice. Usually diplomatic partners carefully select the level of honor they offer each other, depending on various circumstances, the history of the relationship, the principle of reciprocity, political, economic or social necessity, etc. In other words, demonstrating an honor in diplomacy is usually a calculated act. However, there might be cases when the degree of honor to offer becomes a matter of discussion or disagreement in the society. Providing too little honor can humiliate Other, and showing too much honor to Other may insult the collective Self, i.e. be self-embarrassing.

This can be seen in the United Kingdom, which is well known for organizing just one or two stunning state visits of foreign heads of states a year with many spectacular public events. Because of the world-wide attention to such diplomatic events and the level of public attention and respect offered to the guest, often state visits to the United Kingdom become a bone of contention in the country. Tisdall created a list of "controversial and embarrassing guests on state visits" to Britain (2017). Such a sensitive and widely discussed issue has its political aspect and appears as not just an indication of the national sense of Self but also as an element of both domestic and international political bargaining. On January 27, 2017, British Prime Minister Theresa May, on behalf of the Queen Elizabeth II, invited the U.S. President Donald Trump for a state visit, and the invitation was accepted (Reuters 2017 a). However, in a few days "more than 1.3 million people have signed a petition urging the government to call off President Donald Trump's state visit to the UK, amid a row over his recent immigration measures" (BBC News 2017 b).

The degree of demonstration of honor at diplomatic meetings—both verbally and nonverbally—can also be an issue of public, journalistic and scholarly scrutiny. The President of the United States Donald Trump and President of Russia Vladimir Putin had their first and much anticipated meeting on July 7, 2017 during the G-20 summit in Hamburg, Germany. Many news agencies reported that while greeting President Putin, President Trump said "it's an honor to be with you." In a normal diplomatic setting, that can be a standard phrase, but in a tense U.S.-Russian relationship situation affected by the charges of Russia meddling in the American elections, some commentators questioned such a verbal honoring of the Russian President. The Washington Post's headline said: "Meeting Putin was necessary—but hardly 'an honor'" (Editorial Boar 2017). So, in diplomacy, the collective sense of Self can be affected not only by the degree and way of receiving honor from Other but also demonstrating honor to Other. When honoring Other, Self needs to consider the observers—both friends and foes.

The collective sense of Self can be negatively affected when a senior diplomat or another state representative behaves inappropriately abroad. That is an area of the Self's relation with itself in front of Other. For example, a diplomat insults its own country if he or she defects to a foreign state. That is, to say, not only Other but Self can insult itself by turning to Other (insulting alienation).

Former President of Russia Boris Yeltsin was infamous for "surprising" behavior that was perceived as an embarrassment to the Russian collective Self.

> Mr Yeltsin's behaviour has become increasingly bizarre, and might even on occasion be amusing if he were not ultimately responsible for a state with a huge nuclear arsenal and an economy teetering on the brink of total collapse.

> While he has provided entertainment for the world's media, critics say Mr Yeltsin's behaviour has swung between that of a power-junkie and a quixotic figure out of touch with reality.
>
> In 1994 during a visit to Germany, a band struck up a Russian folk song at a champagne luncheon.
>
> The president, in rude health and enjoying the champagne, jumped onto the stage, snatched the baton and conducted the brass band while singing, dancing and blowing kisses to the audience.
>
> A month later, during a Dublin stop-over, Mr Yeltsin was due to meet the Irish premier Albert Reynolds.
>
> After an embarrassingly long wait at the end of a red carpet on the runway at Shannon Airport, the Irish leadership was informed by the president's advisors that he was "unwell" and would not be leaving the plane.
>
> BBC NEWS 1999 A

When discussing symbolic insults in diplomacy in the context of relations between Self and Other, an important question arises: if respect, esteem, honor, dignity and self-regard are so important in diplomacy, why may diplomatic actors try to humiliate their counterparts with an insulting action and risk the existing relationship? To answer this question, we need to understand the nature of diplomatic imperatives—the driving forces of actors involved in international diplomacy.

Diplomatic Imperatives and Symbolic Insult

Self, when it represents the actor's essential political, social, moral or legal being, needs some behavioral imperatives in dealing with Other. Based on the actor's fundamental needs, attitudes, principles and aspirations, these imperatives help the Self to define priorities in a given situation and delineate a policy line in its relations with Other.

An imperative is "an essential or urgent thing," or "a factor or influence making something necessary" (Oxford Dictionaries 2017), "a rule, principle, or need that requires or compels certain action," "a command," "an order" or "obligation" (The American Heritage Dictionary of the English Language 2016), and in diplomacy it instigates diplomatic activities and practices. We define imperative as a motive influenced by policy, and consider diplomatic imperative as a necessitated command willfully accepted by the state for its existence and wellbeing among other international actors.

According to Noé Cornago (2013), the elaboration of diplomacy and diplomatic practices is essentially influenced by such global factors as the development of capitalism, social, institutional, technological, informational and communicational changes. These global factors or forces impose two major—functional and normative—imperatives on diplomacy. For Cornago, diplomatic practices, institutions and discourses have been pluralized under the influence of these imperatives. As a result, the state-centered diplomatic system is transforming to a more pluralistic diplomatic system with the growing role of non-state diplomatic actors and the use of the new and decentralized social and communicational practices. This process also affects the system of states and the state-centered diplomacy forcing them to adapt to the new conditions and get engaged with market capitalist, socio-cultural, social-communication, demographic, technological, environmental and other imperatives of the modern world (Cornago 2013). Indeed, the new global imperatives shape both our understanding of diplomacy and diplomatic practices.

In this paper, we analyze international diplomacy's imperatives to better understand the nature of diplomatic insult. International diplomacy may have various imperatives of political, economic, security, social, moral and legal nature. The political, economic, security and survival related imperatives are based on the actor's crucial interests; social imperatives are built on the sense of community, groupness, relationships and commitments; moral, ethical and justice related imperatives are grounded on certain values and principles; the legal imperatives are supported by law, legitimate rights and agreements. While we distinguish various types of diplomatic imperatives, i.e. imperatives that have an impact on the international activities of states, these imperatives are not cut off from their domestic necessities.

By grouping related diplomatic imperatives, we can differentiate the following four sets: *interest-based, value-based, relationship-based* and *right-based* imperatives. In other words, the state's diplomatic behavior towards other actors can be prompted by its *interests, values, relationships* and *rights*. We can generalize all interest-based imperatives as *political*, value-based imperatives as *moral*, relationship-based imperatives as *social*, and right-based imperatives as *legal* imperatives.

The actor's interests, values, relationships and rights affect its sense of Self, and become parts of its self-concept. Self is not something separated from the actor's interests, values, relationships and rights. Sense of Self is formed in relationship with the actor's identities, needs, attitudes, imperatives and interactions. Within the diplomatic actor's Self, we can also distinguish different but interrelated sub-Selves: the political, moral, social, legal and others. These "sectorial" Selves can be manifested depending on the character of the

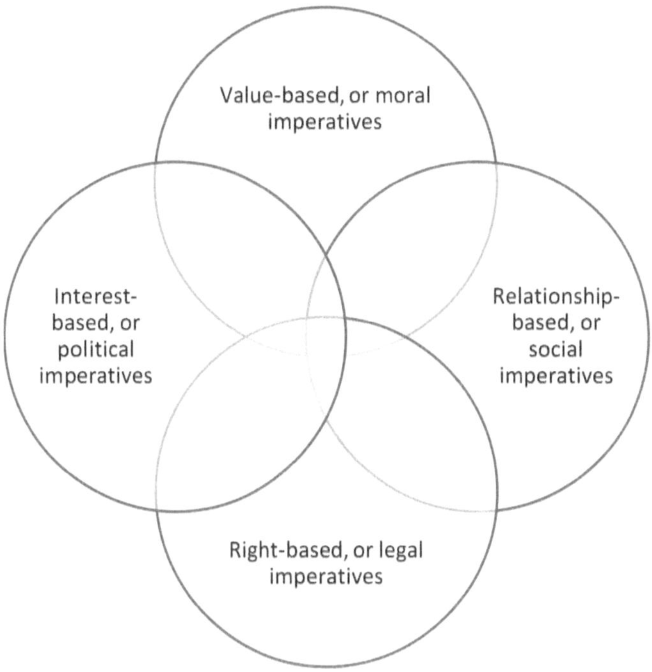

situation or relationship with Other. So, sometimes the actor can show its Self through its political position, and in other situations, it can perform as a moral Self. In a certain period of history, the behavior of the actor can be determined, for example, by its desire to survive, and in another circumstance, it may give preference to the development of cooperation with some other actors, i.e. act as a social Self.

In international diplomacy, all four basic imperatives—interest-based (political), value-based (moral), relationship-based (social) and right-based (legal) imperatives play a role in defining and directing the actor's behavior. These imperatives or combination of them appear to be the most fundamental driving forces of diplomatic actors' behavior. But international law is not free from politics (Reus-Smith 2004), and in international politics legal imperatives are often dependent on actors' interests, values and relationships. Sometimes diplomatic actors may talk about their rights or deny the right of the opponent when that suits their interests, and assume any obligation if that is consistent with their values, and point to certain rights and obligations of other actors, depending on their own relationship with them. For example, in the case of the Crimean crisis of 2014, Russia, on the one hand, and Ukraine and its Western allies, on the other, had diametrically opposed views on the legal

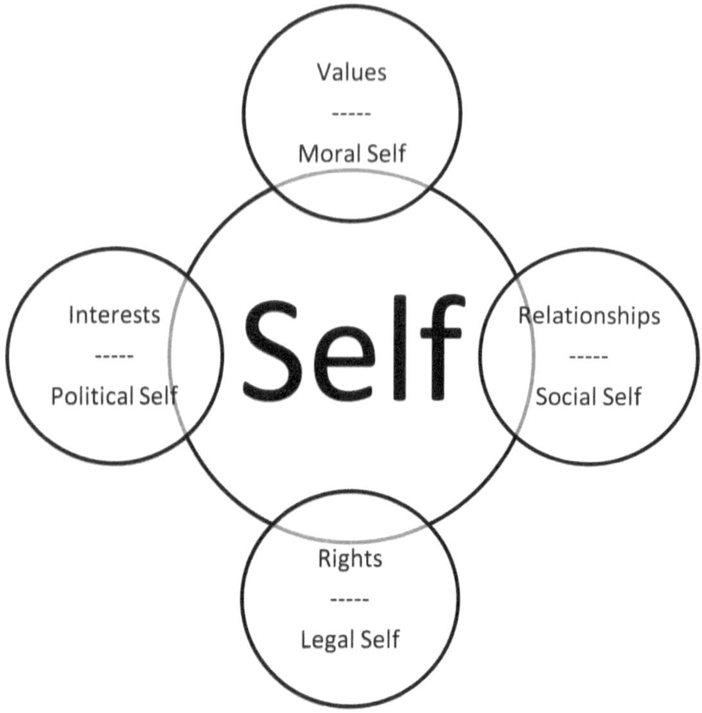

aspects of the change of government in Ukraine as well as interpretation of the legal basis of Kosovo's independence and referendum in Crimea (Faizullaev and Cornut 2017).

International law plays a fundamental role in foundation of diplomatic norms and practices, and making diplomacy as a legitimate institution. It is crucial for organizing and conducting diplomacy, and legal normativity is essential for proper diplomatic practice. Respecting and following international law and conducting diplomacy in the legal framework can help to avoid or reduce diplomatic insults. In fact, diplomatic insult has no legitimacy: according to international law, states have equal rights, and no state-actor have a right to put down or hurt the other actor. But international law defines diplomatic norms and practices not solely: diplomacy has also its interest-based, value-based and relationship-based imperatives that drive the actor's behavior. Symbolic insult in diplomacy has a relation with diplomatic actors' interests and relationships but not rights. Alas, diplomatic actors' moral values are often powerless to resist the pressure of their interest-based imperatives.

Interests, or national interests in the case of international diplomacy, are by far the most recognized factor in explaining the state's foreign policy and

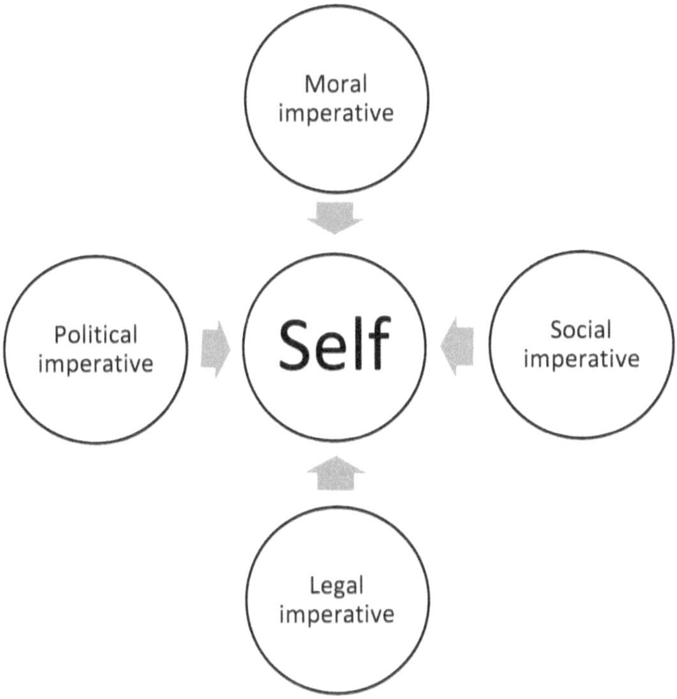

diplomatic behavior. "Interests are needs, desires, concerns, fears—the things one cares about or wants" (Ury, Brett and Goldberg 1993: 5). In international theory, the realist tradition tends to have a "materialist" view on the national interests (Wendt 1999: 114). The constructivist approach goes beyond that and includes social factors. According to Wendt, national interests can be related not only to physical survival, autonomy, and economic well-being, as George and Keohane indicated (1980: 217–238), but also to a collective self-esteem—"a group's need to feel good about itself, for respect or status" (1999: 236). Wendt defines national interests "as the objective interests of state-society complexes, consisting of four needs: physical survival, autonomy, economic well-being, and collective self-esteem" (1999: 198).

In our opinion, we can approach national interests in a wider and a narrower sense. In the wider sense, national interests can include not only needs such as physical survival, autonomy, economic well-being and collective self-esteem, but also the actor's values, relationships and rights since all these factors are essential for the functioning and development of the state/nation in an international environment. But in the narrower sense, we can link national interests with such basic, objective and primarily material needs as survival, security, economic well-being and development. Apart from these traditional areas of essential political concerns, states may have values, relationships and rights that can exist not only in cohesion, but in certain contradiction with the above mentioned basic, objective and mostly material needs. In other words, not every aspect of the diplomatic actor's behavior can be explained by its interests: there are some other things—values, relations and rights/ obligations—which determinate the behavior of Self. As well, the actor's (political) interests, (moral) values, (social) relations and (legal) rights/obligations may not always coincide with each other. For example, country A may criticize country B for human right violations, but at the same time, it sells the latter military equipment.

Values, relationships and rights are also crucial for the state's existence and development, and they can influence the actor's understanding of its national interests. All needs and imperatives have their objective and subjective sides, but value-based, relationship-based and right-based imperatives are relatively more subjective and exposed to the influence of social factors, including the personal convictions of the political decision makers.

The actor's sense of Self relates to all the factors we mentioned above: the interests, values, relationships and rights. The Self's ontological security also depends on how protected its interests, values, relations and rights are. Self, as an essential and integral being or conglomerate of the actor's political, moral, social and legal Selves, is weakened if one of its essential segments is damaged. A state may have a nuclear weapon, protected borders and economic well-being, but if it is not respected internationally, its Self always would have deficiency and would feel ontological insecurity.

At the same time, when the integral sense of Self is hurt, the actor's particular—political, moral, social and legal Selves can be deteriorated. Self and sense of Self cannot be separated from the actor's political, moral, social and legal stances. Therefore, in our analysis we consider Self as a certain derivative of the actor's interest-based, value-based, relationship-based and right-based needs and aspirations. Self's feeling and seeing itself in certain social environments, i.e. its sense of Self, self-concept and self-regard, depends not only on general recognition and esteem of the Self by Other(s), but also on the social status of its specific interests, values, relationships and rights. If the state A publicly and diplomatically acknowledges the state B as an equal, respected and honorable partner but nevertheless captures a part of B's land or offends the religious feelings of its citizens, or insults its national hero, it is unlikely that B will experience ontological security in front of A.

We can approach collective self-esteem as a separate need of the state as a social actor, as a part of its national interest, as Wendt (1999) suggested. We can also recognize the pursuit of honor and interest as primary motives in international relations, as Lebow (2016) suggested. However, we can go further and consider self-regard as an organic part of the actor's total basic imperatives. The diplomatic actor's self-regard is a necessity that relates to its physical survival, autonomy and economic well-being as well as to its core values, social relations and fundamental rights. The actor's self-regard depends on the status of all its basic needs and aspirations. When the state acts as a diplomatic actor, i.e. interacts with other international actors in accordance with diplomatic norms and observing diplomatic culture, its interest-based, value-based, relationship-based and right-based imperatives are linked with its self-regard, and they mutually affect each other. That means, by defending the socially supported sense of Self or self-regard, the actor defends its political, moral, social and legal needs and aspirations; and vice versa. When Self defends its political, moral, social and legal needs and aspirations, it protects its self-regard. That also means that by affecting the actor's sense of Self, particularly self-regard, Other can affect its political, moral, social and legal Selves or stances.

Collective or national self-regard exists as an essential aspect or component of the diplomatic actor's existence and sense of Self. Collective self-regard relates to international status of the actor's interests, values, relationships and

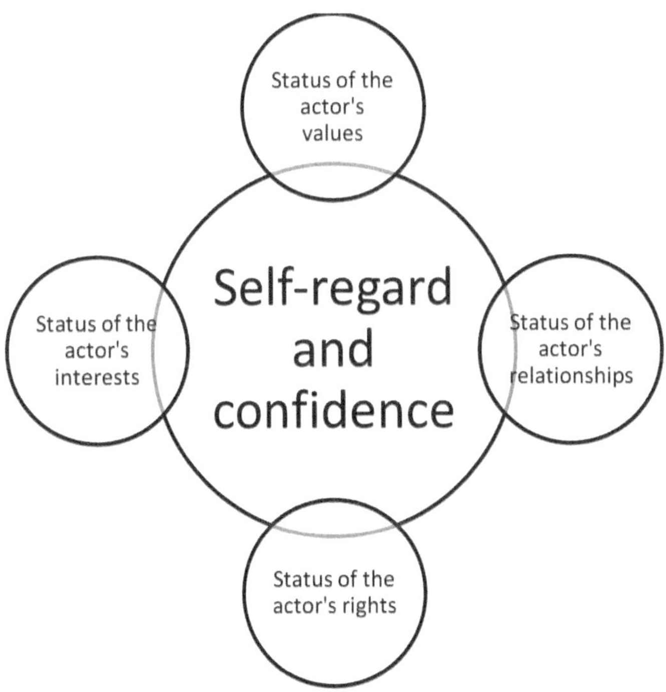

rights. Political resources, moral authority, the strength of social ties, and recognition of rights are the important sources of the diplomatic actors' power and self-confidence.

As far as value-based imperatives of diplomacy go, they are subsequent to the state's moral stance, human rights, humanitarian and other principal and decent convictions. Diplomatic practices of states that are constituted in religious principles, may be affected by some religious/spiritual values. The state may have a moral purpose (Reus-Smith 1999), and it chooses morally oriented international behavior when it relies on its value-based imperative. Apparently, different diplomatic actors can challenge each other's core values or disagree with them since states may have disparate understandings of moral, ethical and spiritual issues and decency. Even when certain moral values, for example, democracy, human rights or gender equality, are important for different states, they can get into disagreement in assessing each other's intentions and behavior because of the differences in seeing the status of these values in their value-system.

A relationship-based imperative comes from the social nature and roots of diplomacy, the existence of "diplomatic relations" between states and the necessity of interactions among diplomatic actors for their survival, cohabitation and well-being. The Vienna Convention on Diplomatic Relations (1961)—the basic document regulating the conduct of modern diplomacy—considers the development of *friendly relations between nations* as the main objective of international diplomacy. "*Diplomacy makes relations*" (Bjola and Kornprobst 2013: 113), and relational contexts shape diplomatic practices (Cornut 2017). Bjola (2013) suggested putting "relationship management" at the center of diplomatic studies and considered diplomacy as a method of managing relations of enmity and friendship in world politics. Though, he pointed out, "little is known about how relationships of enmity and friendship are made and unmade in international politics" (2013: 9). When we say "relationship", we mean social relationship, or the status of social relations. The social environment and need for relationship management leads to the actors' socially oriented behavior.

States can stand on their interests, or values, or relationships, or rights, or combination of them in going to war or maintaining peace, and acting and interacting internationally. Certain imperatives may have an altered significance in diplomatic activities of different states. Various imperatives can also dissimilarly influence the state's foreign policy and international politics in distinct circumstances. Diplomatic imperatives may get into diverse types of relations. For example, building relationships with a particular state can serve political or other interests of the state but contradict its moral stance, or the state can consciously worsen its relations with other states in order to advance its military interests, or the state's business interests and moral impetuses can hamper each other. The state's basic imperatives could support each other, or the actor can try to get certain congruence or balance among them. Thus, the state's diplomatic behavior can be based on a kind of complimentary mixture of its interests, values, and relationships as well as rights, obligations and commitments.

However, the state can be honest or manipulative in explaining its diplomatic imperatives. It may openly admit its real interests, value stance and relationship goals, but it may also describe its international behavior by referring to one imperative, for example, to moral obligations, but in reality, it can act according to political expediency. Sometimes it is very difficult to clarify the actual cause of the state's behavior because of the complexity and mixture of objective and subjective factors affecting international politics. Thus, despite the extensive debates about the true reasons for the U.S. invasion of Iraq in 2003, there is no clear answer to this query. So, the real driving force of an action of the state and its explanation could coincide or mismatch. Actors' and observers' cognitive biases, believes and attribution errors can also contribute to the diversities in explanation of international behavior. These are some of the reasons why analyses and explanations of international behavior of states can be so interpretative and controversial.

Countries can maintain or develop relationships to achieve some strategic objectives or advance certain values, but they can also build relationships for the sake of relationships too, because relationships with the international community may also represent an asset for them. In other words, relationship itself can occur as a certain value, and valuable relations have a bigger motivational impact than insignificant ones. For example, one of the main reasons of the United Kingdom's support of the U.S. invasion of Iraq was the UK government's strong relationship imperative towards the United States. Well before this invasion and completion of the UN weapon inspectors' work in Iraq, the British Prime Minister Tony Blair wrote to the American President George W. Bush "I will be with you, whatever" (The Report of the Iraq Inquiry 2016: 15). Of course, such a relationship oriented attitude can be supported by the actor's interests and values, or built on both interests and values. Relationship can also be seen as interest and/or value, and value and relationship can be realized as interest, and interest and value may appear as building blocks of relationship. Nevertheless, the relationship with the United States was the first and foremost factor in Tony Blair's decision to invade Iraq. The "special relations" narrative refers to countries as unitary and purposive actors. Speaking about Theresa May as the next British Prime Minister, the White House Press Secretary Josh Earnest noted that President Obama continues "to rest on the principle that the relationship between the United States and the United Kingdom is a special one, and it is a relationship that transcends the personalities or political parties of either country's leader" (2016).

Often, relations between states are affected by their concrete activities and accomplishments in different areas, for instance, their human rights records, or political stance, or economic achievements, and so on. When state A provides humanitarian assistance or political support to state B, that act influences state B's relationship with state A. Relations between state C and state D may deteriorate, if state D threatens or occupies the territory of state E which has close political and economic relations with state C. So, relationships between states immensely depend on their actions and attitudes significant to both. In this respect, making war and peace between nations are the major causes of interstate relationship.

Although the actor's actions are functions of its convictions, diplomatic actors' real performances may have a reversed impact on their imperatives. Thus, not only imperatives form practices but practices also influence or reshape imperatives. It is hard for state A to voice human rights concerns regarding state B, if A has a poor human rights record itself.

Diplomats may be seen "as agents of cooperation among states" (Cross 2007: 1), but they may also act as agents of competition and even war, or those who pursue just selfish interests of their states. Diplomats can fulfill humanitarian missions and advance moral values, and be involved in devious actions of their governments. In general, the development of the relationship with other international actors is one of the prime objectives of diplomacy, but a diplomatic actor may also pursue its interest-related and value-related goals in the first place by keeping normative relationships at a low level.

Thus, by defending or advancing its interest internationally, a state can offend—deliberately or involuntarily—an opponent. However, as a diplomatic actor, Self needs to maintain relationship with Other, even with an outspoken opponent—that is a way of diplomacy, i.e. influencing through communication, negotiation and persuasion. In this case, a diplomatic actor can intentionally apply a mild, often symbolic insult against its opponent to weaken the other side's Self, but at the same time to maintain relationship with Other. By lowering an opponent's self-regard and threatening its ontological security, an offender may have a better opportunity to advance its interests vis-à-vis a weakened opponent. But because of the ambiguity of symbolic insult, that kind of action may allow an actor to look innocent and continue the relationship with the opponent. Symbolic insult, in this case, appears as a diplomatic instrument that allows for the maintenance of a balance between Self's s interests and relationships in interactions with the opposing Other.

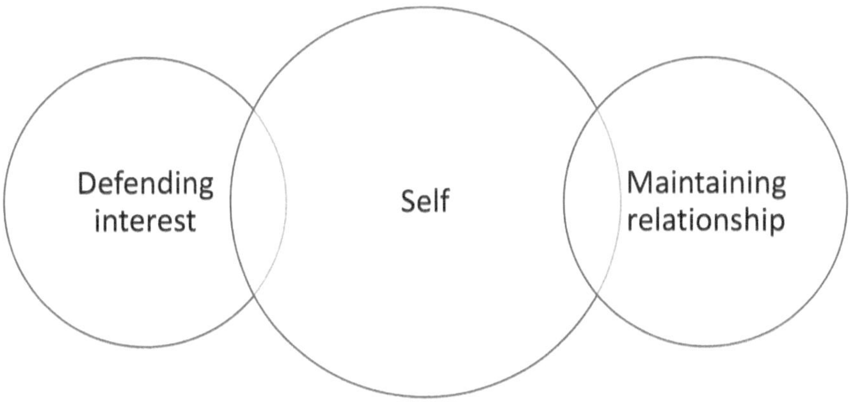

Symbolic Insult in Diplomacy as a Manipulative Practice

Despite the importance of diplomatic tactfulness and respect, there might also be "calculated breach of diplomatic norms about civility" (Sharp 2009: 206). Diplomacy is a civilized, legally established and culturally refined activity, but it may use different forms of manipulation, including cheating with the use of symbols (Faizullaev 2013: 112–113). Symbolic insult as a subtle way of weakening the opponent without the rupture of the relationship is one of the forms of political and social manipulation. To be "effective", such a manipulative act should be "unnoticeable" but comprise a hidden message—a concealed assault on the actor's sense of Self. Obscurity and ambiguity can be an instrument of manipulation, a sign of hypocrisy.

There might be many reasons for deception, and that is a large area of social, psychological and political studies. Our point here is that diplomatic manipulations can be related to the conflict between the actor's interest-based and relationship-based imperatives, or political and social aspirations in relations with the opponent. Oddly enough, elusive forms of symbolic insult, which is intended to advance the Self's interests by staying engaged with Other, can appear as one of the methods—although subtle and manipulative—of managing relations of enmity and friendship in international politics, what Bjola has said (2013).

Strategic Gamesmanship and Manipulations

The study of political manipulations is not new in the tradition of political thought. In ancient China, rulers, politicians, generals and diplomats widely practiced *stratagems*—"an artifice or trick in war for deceiving and outwitting the enemy" (Merriam-Webster Dictionary 2017). However, the famous ancient

Chinese 36 stratagems were considered not just a deception but necessary strategic skills in dealing with others in war, politics, diplomacy and even everyday life (von Senger 1993). One of the stratagems related to the topic of this paper is "Hide a knife behind a smile"—in the context of our paper, "knife" for advancing Self's interests, and "smile" for keeping its relationships with the Other.

Stratagems represent the art of survival, defending vital interests, solving problems and achieving goals in military, politics, diplomacy and everyday life by being more strategically effective than the adversary. Sun Tzu's famous "Art of War" (2002)—an ancient Chinese tract on military strategy—is a classic example of using a stratagem approach for defeating the enemy. Deceiving and cunning emerge as a natural part of strategic interactions in a military confrontation. But the use of tricks in politics, diplomacy and everyday life raises many questions of a moral nature. As Harro von Senger wrote in his seminal book on 36 Chinese stratagems (1993), since ancient time people in China have understood stratagem not as an immoral practice, but rather as the art of canning for finding and using unorthodox and unconventional ways to deal with hostile people. While in the West cunning was criminalized and renounced, in China it was seen as a sign of wisdom and a useful skill of problem solving. And yet in the West, noted von Senger, cunning is also used widely—but more instinctively and silently. Here is what The Telegraph wrote on this matter: "In the West such strategies are often regarded as unethical" and "Chinese perceptions of what is right and wrong are often quite different from ours"; "However, if one is realistic about the West, are our ethics really any different, even if the packaging and presentation are gentler?" (2004).

As von Senger pointed out, Western philosophy, ethics and morality traditionally resisted to discuss cunning as a useful strategic skill (perhaps, Machiavellism is the well-known exception), although Ancient Greek mythology was more tolerant for those who applied tricks and manipulations in their counteraction with adversaries (for example, Odyssey was admired for his cunning). Fairy tales also are quite positive about the characters who use deceit and cunning in confronting the evil forces and achieving noble goals. Deception, bluff, cheating, trickery, falsehood, misleading, dishonesty, fraud, lying and the similar concepts naturally cause our dislike: they are unacceptable from moral (value), social (relationship) and legal (law) points of view. However, in a military confrontation, deception might be seen as a natural means for the saving life, survival and victory over the enemy. But various forms of manipulation also become a part of political life where the actors can defend and promote their—often conflicting—interests. Apparently, political actors may have common interests, or they can overcome the differences in their interests by finding or constructing some other shared interests or values, or on the basis of good will, development of positive relationships and law. Nevertheless, diplomacy as an instrument of foreign policy and international politics, can be driven by the interest-based imperative, and diplomatic actors may be tempted to use manipulative means in their efforts to protect national interests, or defend their ontological security.

Many outstanding authors such as Francois de Callieres (2010), Jules Cambon (1931) and Harold Nicolson (1939) wrote about the value of honesty in diplomacy. Indeed, honesty, sincerity and truthfulness are the virtues of diplomacy and diplomats. But it is hard to imagine manipulation-free and insult-free diplomacy, when countries are focused on the advancement of their national interests, states have their secrets, spies covertly work as diplomats, and diplomatic actors may pursue hidden political and strategic objectives. However, strengthening the role of moral, social and legal imperatives in diplomacy as well as dissemination of good practices can help in the development of honest and transparent diplomatic practices.

Stratagemic moves in diplomacy, or diplomatic gamesmanship can be a feature of diplomatic insulting reciprocities. When they experience an apparent insult, diplomatic actors often use "tit-for-tat" retaliation. That is a usual practice when one country expels diplomats of another state from its territory. However, a country whose diplomats were expelled, can chose another, more ambiguous move. For instance, on December 29, 2016, President of the U.S. Barack Obama decided to expel 35 Russian diplomats over the U.S. presidential election hacking allegation. But Russian President Vladimir Putin decided not to retaliate with the same action.[20] That strategic move was judged differently. Incoming President Donald Trump assessed this political gesture of Putin as "very smart" (Allen, Oliphant and Foster 2016). Some observers saw this step as a very strong answer, or even insult to Barack Obama. "Putin Zings Obama With Vicious Historical Insult", wrote Mikhail Klikushin in the Observer (2017). "President Vladimir Putin castigated the United States on Friday for imposing sanctions and expelling Russian diplomats amid allegations of Russian

20 Russia announced its retaliation on 28 July, 2017 after the U.S. Congress approved new sanctions on Russia (The Ministry of Foreign Affairs of Russian Federation 2017). The Russian response included reducing the number of American diplomatic and technical staff in Russia to 455, and closing the U.S. Embassy summer residence and canceling the access to its warehouse. The next move was from the United States. On August 31, 2017, the U.S. State Department issued a press statement: "In the spirit of parity invoked by the Russians, we are requiring the Russian Government to close its Consulate General in San Francisco, a chancery annex in Washington, D.C., and a consular annex in New York City" (Nauert 2017).

meddling in the American presidential election, but said no U.S. diplomats will be ousted in reprisal for President Barack Obama's moves in the wake of hacking attacks", noted Josh Lederman and Nataliya Vasilyeva of the Associated Press (2016). Here is a former CNN Moscow Bureau Chief and Russian analyst's opinion: "Putin's "extraordinary" move essentially sidelines the Obama administration while it is still in office, said CNN's former Moscow bureau chief and Russia analyst Jill Dougherty. By not responding to the challenge thrown down by Washington with tit-for-tat measures, as a Russian president normally would have to do, Putin is really issuing "an enormous insult" to Obama, she said" (CNN Wire 2016). An actor may gain stratagemic and manipulative opportunities, when it keeps an option to retaliate but doesn't "open its cards" in strategic interactions with the opponent.

Discussing political manipulations in European traditions, we may recall, for example, Niccolò Machiavelli's "The Prince". It is noteworthy that there is a special chapter in this treatise on how flatterers should be avoided because flattery can be misleading about the real interests and intentions of the flatterer. Diplomatic language can be subtle, understated, sophisticated, nuanced and polite but diplomats develop excellent communication skills and usually perfectly understand each other (Langholtz 2004: 14–15). However, the need for both clearness and ambiguity of diplomatic language provides opportunities for linguistic manipulations, and that may require from diplomats multi-layered work with coding and decoding meanings.

Thomas Schelling (1960) and Erving Goffman (1969) proposed two original ways of studying manipulative behavior which could be linked to the study of stratagems/cunnings and the Machiavellian manipulative behavior. Schelling analyzed the strategy and tactics of commitments, promises and threats in the context of bargaining and in relation to game theory (game of strategy). We will return to Schelling's view when we discuss the relations between tacit bargaining and concealed insult.

Goffman's approach and major concepts such as dramaturgical presentation of Self in everyday life, face-work, stigma, ritual and frame analyses are closely connected to the study of symbolic interactions. Goffman also approached calculated strategic interaction from the game perspective (1969). He remarked: "Whenever students of the human scene have considered the dealings individuals have with one another, the issue of calculation has arisen: When a respectable motive is given for action, are we to suspect an ulterior one?" (1969: 85). Discussing strategic interactions between individuals, Goffman mentioned diplomacy. "Not surprisingly, literature on diplomacy stresses these gamesman qualities, since diplomats may have to represent parties of great importance in situations where minor interaction gains can have great consequence" (Goffman 1969: 85). Later, we will discuss one of symbolic and strategic interactions Goffman analyzed—"face-work" with its essential consequences for both individual and diplomatic actors' sense of Self.

In modern political theory, political manipulations have been systematically studied by William Riker (1986). Ricker coined the word "heresthetics" which "refers to the manipulation of the decision situation so that participants decide as the manipulator desires, despite an initial disinclination to do so" (1995, 34). In his writing, Riker has shown that agenda control, framing, introducing new dimensions of the issue of concern and other heresthetical practices are often used both in domestic and international politics.

Political manipulations, however, may refer to a wide range of activities, including strategic communication and negotiation. By using the theory of heresthetics, Erik Voeten examined the practice of political manipulation in the context of collective bargaining in international organizations, including bargaining over self-determination (2011). Despite the fact that political manipulations of diplomatic actors in international organizations, for example, through voting, can cause the opposite side displeasure (Voeten 2011: 272), not all such actions threaten an opponent's sense of Self—the very fact of the social self-existence.

In a diplomatic context, Self can be threatened through the lowering of its social status and significance. As we already pointed out, one of the most substantial threats for diplomatic actors is the danger of indecency, dishonor of Self. If soldiers can lose their self-regard in a battle, the endangerment for the diplomatic actor's Self is humiliation. Any humiliation of the collective actor's Self is also a disgrace of the Selves of the people who identify themselves with this "grandeur" Self. That is the case, especially, for those who represent diplomatic actors internationally—head of states and governments, foreign ministers, ambassadors or even lower ranking diplomats.

Diplomacy may use many honest practices aimed at ensuring security, international peace, understanding and prosperity. Diplomatic actors can decently communicate, negotiate, make joint agreements and try to solve international problems. But they can also lie or use some form of manipulation to influence other international actors and achieve their political, economic or other objectives. Not only following the rules but also breaking them (Kuus 2014) as well as diplomats' improvisations within the set of rules and norms (Cornut 2017) may be a part of diplomatic strategic skills. Deliberative symbolic insult—hurting the other side's sense of Self through a symbolically meaningful and emotionally saturated act—is a manipulative activity, and diplomatic actors who apply such an action may openly deny any wrongdoing. Ambiguity of diplomatic language and signaling (Cohen 1981; Jonsson and Aggestam 1999) creates a suitable ground for such manipulations.

Representational Manipulation

Diplomacy occurs through representation: diplomats, envoys as well as embassies and diplomatic missions represent the state or other international entities. Representation in diplomacy has a strong symbolic aspect because diplomats symbolize those whom they represent. Therefore, one of the most widespread symbolic manipulations in diplomacy is representational manipulation. The appointment of an envoy is always considered a highly symbolic act: with this action, countries express some meaning and can please or upset each other. Country A can feel displeasure or annoyance when country B appoints an inconvenient ambassador to its capital.[21] State C can reject a proposed ambassador from state D, or give an *agrément* after a very long consideration thus indicating their reluctance. As a part of a wider bargaining process, state E can delay an appointment of its ambassador to state F for an uncertain period. As a reaction to the appointment of a somewhat undesirable ambassador of state G to its capital, state H may only send a charge d'affairs to state G. Diplomatic actors can use the raising or lowering of the level of diplomatic representation, including delegations to international conferences and meetings, as a means of a wider and multi-faceted bargaining process—to get something from the other side with some apparent or tacit pressure. Non-recognition, boycott, isolation, sanctions, recalling an ambassador, and lowering the level of communication and representation are among the strongest diplomatic insulting tactics which may negatively affect the adversary's sense of Self.

Media and Social Media Manipulations

Since nonverbal forms of symbolism is widely used in diplomacy, diplomatic actors can employ symbolic insult nonverbally. Electronic revolution has made nonverbal communication in diplomacy particularly salient (Cohen 1987: 212). Using social media in diplomacy has opened new opportunities for symbolic manipulative actions and interactions. For example, a foreign ministry or embassy could deliver to the public a meaningful message on its Facebook page that may not be entirely an official point of view. Sometimes such a message may have multiple meanings or even contain a symbolic strike or rebuke.

21 On May 14, 2014, Newsweek reacted to the appointment of a new American Ambassador to Russia with the following headline: "Ambassador Tefft Would Upset Russia, and That's the Point" (Browning 2015).

Lowering collective self-esteem is a risky act: it may hurt feelings of the people who identify themselves with the collective being. That can also cause a retaliatory action. But diplomatic actors can use media and social media for an indirect insult. For example, on September 3, 2014, the United States Diplomacy Center held its groundbreaking ceremony. The website of the center described that event: "In a historic gathering, Secretary of State John Kerry and 5 former Secretaries of State—Kissinger, Baker, Albright, Powell, and Clinton—united for the groundbreaking ceremony for the U.S. Diplomacy Center. After giving remarks in the Department of State's Marshall Center auditorium, the Secretaries walked outside to the construction site for the groundbreaking in honor of the future museum" (United States Diplomacy Center 2014). Additionally, the U.S. Diplomacy Center's website published the photo of the Secretaries of State at that ceremony. On September 8, 2014, the Russian foreign ministry's Facebook page re-published this photo with the following remark: "Let's hope that this is not the mobilization of veterans on digging out trenches of the Cold War" (Russian Foreign Ministry's Facebook page 2014). Whilst the intention of the message may have been lighthearted and comical, it certainly could be perceived by the other side and observers as a caustic remark or even insult because of the prejudiced interpretation of a symbolically significant event.

In similar circumstances, diplomatic actors can easily enter into a manipulative game of symbolic insult. They may also be unwittingly involved in scandals over controversial movies and cartoons since the latter, even if created by private individuals, can be perceived by other parties as extremely insulting wrongdoings which hurt national or religious sense of Self. Even awarding a prize to an individual by an independent organization could be perceived as a diplomatic offence since an award, especially an internationally recognized one, has an important symbolic meaning. According to Marc Lanteigne, the 2010 Nobel Peace Prize to jailed political activist Liu Xiaobo was treated by Beijing "as a diplomatic insult by Norway, even though the award process is independent from government" (2013, 80).

Media may become an instrument in diplomatic confrontation when it is totally controlled by the state. For example, after unanimous adoption by the UN Security Council, new sanctions were placed on North Korea in response to its ballistic missile tests on July 4 and 28, 2017. In response "'North Korean state media has slammed the latest round of sanctions approved by the United Nations, calling them a "flagrant violation of our sovereignty." It vowed retaliation against Washington" (CNN Wire Service 2017). That is the usual diplomatic language of Pyongyang and it hardly surprised anyone in the world.

Symbolic Insult in Digital Diplomacy

Disinformation and information warfare are as old as the world itself. But today we are witnessing electronic warfare, cyberwarfare, Photoshop and social media manipulations. Online insults and humiliations are part of this struggle. Internet trolling, fake photos and the distortion of online images can affect people's perceptions and political judgments. "Fake news" has become a part of political discourse. If Nazi and Stalinist propaganda was "black" and "white" in its content, i.e. clearly differentiated "good" and "evil", modern manipulations of images can be subtler and influence people subconsciously. However, with the use of contemporary technologies, adversaries can create very unattractive, ugly images of politicians. For example, we can analyze "enemy images" of some American politicians in Iranian or North Korean media, and some Iranian and North Korean politicians in the American media.

However, with the spread of digital diplomacy, we can also see a new phenomenon: digital diplomatic insults committed by diplomatic actors. Foreign ministries and embassies are mostly involved in such an activity not through their official websites but through social media accounts. That allows them to be more flexible and creative. During a tense political situation, the opposite sides can use more inflammatory language and images. Nations can use social media for framing world events and other governments to promote their foreign policies (Manor 2014). Ilan Manor analyzed how Russia and the United States narrated one another's character by framing each other on social media (2015). In doing so, he pointed out, they tried to morally de-legitimize each other, and such a practice represents a form of symbolic violence which "may be relevant to the field of diplomacy in general, and digital diplomacy in particular" (Manor 2015). Sherzod Arapov (2016) analyzed Russian and Turkish foreign ministries' and other official bodies' 262 tweets published before and after the downing of the Russian military airplane (Su-24) by Turkey on November 24, 2015. In this intergovernmental Twitter clash, the opponents tried to symbolically violate each other's legitimacy and morality. However, in more ordinary situations diplomatic actors may use more subtle forms of symbolic insult. But still, "technology has made diplomacy less diplomatic and information warfare less subtle" (Taylor 2017). As evidence, Adam Taylor refers to the Twitter account of the Russian Embassy in London. "In recent years, the account has gained global fame for its sardonic tweets. Generally, these messages seemed less about projecting Moscow's policies abroad and more about criticizing the apparent hypocrisy of the United States and Europe" (Taylor 2017). In his article, Taylor analyzed "the seven most popular tweets from the account, which offer a glimpse of tactics the Russian Embassy uses to criticize the West". Interestingly, one of the comments under Taylor's article noted that "couldn't the Russians say exactly the same thing about Voice of America?".

Alex Luhn also analyzed the same Embassy tweets in the article entitled "Russian embassy's Twitter account vents barbs against west" (2017). Here are some of the Embassy tweets and Luhn's remarks about them:

> "It is deplorable that @BorisJohnson found himself unfit to stand Western ground on Syria in bilateral talks with Sergey Lavrov," the embassy said, in reference to the foreign secretary cancelling a planned visit to Moscow while US secretary of state Rex Tillerson goes ahead with his.
>
> It illustrated the tweet with a painting of the charge of the Light Brigade, when Russian gunners decimated British cavalry during the Crimean war.
>
> "If G7 ultimatum to Russia brings us to real war, what is your trust in @realDonaldTrump as a wartime leader & @BorisJohnson as his lieutenant?" it asked followers in a mocking Twitter poll.
>
> After Barack Obama expelled 35 Russian diplomats over accusations of Russian hacking during the US election, it tweeted a picture of a duck with the word "lame" superimposed on top of it, and said that everybody "will be glad to see the last of this hapless" administration.
>
> In January, it included a picture Pepe the Frog—a cartoon so beloved by the alt-right that the Anti-Defamation League has listed it as a hate symbol—in a tweet referencing Theresa May.
>
> LUHN 2017

Russian Prime Minister Dmitry Medvedev also joined the social media attacks against President Obama. "It is regrettable that the Obama administration, which started out by restoring our ties, is ending its term in an anti-Russia agony. RIP" (CNN Wire Service 2016).

Apparently, any diplomatic social media accounts targets both political elites and the general audience. Luhn referred to the opinion of Charlie Beckett, media and communications professor at the London School of Economics, who "said the embassy account had found a ready audience among users who were already skeptical of the west" (2017). As professor Beckett put it, "the Russian embassy could get away with provocative tweets because of the country's misinformation campaign and claims of being a victim of western aggression (Luhn 2017).

Some heated diplomatic Twitter exchanges have become well-known. One of them is the Twitter engagement between Canadian and Russian Missions to NATO in August 27 and 28, 2014. RT called this a "tweet-for-tat war" (2014), and Times referred to it as "the Canada-Russia tweet battle" (Burnett 2014). A Canadian tweet from August 27 offered a geography lesson to the Russian side: "Geography can be tough. Here's a guide for Russian soldiers who keep getting lost & 'accidentally' entering #Ukraine". "The snide post, which includes labels of "Russia" and "Not Russia," was aimed at the Kremlin's soldiers who "keep getting lost & 'accidentally' entering #Ukraine"—a clear reference to the recent capture of Russian soldiers in Ukrainian territory" (Burnett 2014). But the next day the Russian delegation published its own caustic rebuttal: "Helping our Canadian colleagues to catch up with contemporary geography of #Europe." The Russian tweet offered a map where the Crimean Peninsula belonged to Russia.

On November 13, 2017, the British Prime Minister Theresa May in a speech at the Lord Mayor's Banquet in London "mounted a stern attack on Russia, claiming that it interferes in elections and plants fake news stories to sow discord and undermine Western institutions" (Grinberg and Mortensen 2017). Particularly, she said: "I have a very simple message for Russia. We know what you are doing. And you will not succeed. Because you underestimate the resilience of our democracies, the enduring attraction of free and open societies, and the commitment of Western nations to the alliances that bind us" (Rowena 2017). In resonse, Russian Foreign Ministry published an official comment of its spokesperson Maria Zakharova with condemning Theresa May for "irresponsible and groundless nature of accusations against Russia" and blaming London for "fundamental incomprehension of current processes in the world and of the essence of the very UN Charter-based international legal order that the United Kingdom is vowing to protect" (Zakharova 2017). Some Russian politicians also made critical statements about the speech of the UK Prime Minister, and all these recriminations quite fit into the canons of international political confrontation. But in the context of this paper the Russian foreign ministry's twit with the photo of Teresa May drinking red wine and the image of a glass of red wine, is even more remarkable: #UK Prime Minister @theresa_may on @Russia: "We know what you are doing". We know what YOU are doing as well. Dear Theresa, we hope, one day you will try Crimean #Massandra red wine" (Russian Foreign Ministry's Twitter page 2017). Despite a certain jocularity and seeming harmlessness, this tweet may be even more insulting than the official tough statement. It is sardonic, condescending and mocking. However, at the same time the tweet is not so uppity to provoke the British side on serious political responses. In short, it presents a subtle diplomatic insult which makes a political point but doesn't burn bridges.

Usually these kinds of tweets use sardonic language, sarcasm, mockery and other forms of mainly indirect insulting. However, recently a senior Russian diplomat—a deputy Ambassador to the United Nations—Vladimir Safronkov surprised everyone with his quite undiplomatic speech at the UN Security Council. "Accusing the British of blocking political efforts to end the Syrian conflict, the Russian deputy envoy to the United Nations suddenly wagged a finger at Matthew Rycroft, Britain's permanent representative to the United Nations, and said: "Look at me! Don't you look away from me! Why are you looking away?" "Don't you dare insult Russia again," he added later. Safronkov's tone, not just what he said but how he said it, turned heads" (Roth 2017). An important element of Safronkov's intervention was his "unusual use of the familiar "you" ("ty" in Russian, as opposed to the formal "vy"), which is "used for talking to friends and children and almost never in public addresses" (Roth 2017).

In Russia, public opinion about Safronkov's behavior—mostly expressed on social media—was divided: some people considered it as shameful, but others strongly supported it. Some Internet memes were published in social media. Kremlin spokesman Dmitry Peskov was supportive by saying to reporters that "Nothing offensive was said. Manifestations of the spinelessness are fraught in the future with deplorable consequences. Therefore, it is better to defend the interests of our homeland today, and, if necessary, in a rather tough manner" (Sputnik 2017 b). RT, Russian international television network, presented this incident in more political terms, in part by moving the arrow on the British envoy: "Speaking earlier in front of the 15-member circle, Britain's envoy Matthew Rycroft accused Moscow of supporting "*a murderous, barbaric criminal*"—Syrian President Bashar Assad—"*rather than with their international peers*". The envoy also stated that sarin, a nerve gas, had been found at the site of last week's alleged government-orchestrated chemical attack on a rebel-controlled area in the north of the country" (RT 2017).

According to Vladislav Inozemtsev (2017), in a situation of continued deterioration of relations between Russia and the West, the language and the tone of statements of Russian diplomats and other officials has become less diplomatic and impolite while their Western counterparts' has remained unchanged. But we may expect that both sides may blame each other for such a deterioration and provide some examples of insulting behavior of the Other. Diplomatic standoffs can be seen at different levels, and their explanation is usually highly interpretative. Social networks and digital diplomacy have brought even more complications to this area by bringing new elements of informational manipulation. U.S. President Trump's twitter diplomacy is one of the most controversial phenomenon in this respect. "Trump's diplomacy-by-Twitter sets off firestorm", is the headline of the article of Rebecca Kheel and Ellen Mitchel in The Hill (2017). Hillary Clinton criticized President Trump's

Twitter diplomacy, "warning that it's ineffective in pressing North Korea to stop its saber-rattling" (McCaskill 2017). With his twits and gaffes, President Trump "has earned almost universal disapproval from the political and especially the diplomatic establishments, which regard such heedless commentary as, first, ill-advised in the extreme and, second, plain crass" (Dejensky 2017). However, as Mary Dejensky states, "diplomacy itself might benefit from more straight talking", and "already, despite all the criticism, it is possible to observe a Trump effect rubbing off on international discourse. We are hearing a new immediacy and outspokenness that used to be exclusive to the likes of Nigel Farage" (2017). But diplomacy is a field where collective Selves interact, and there is a significant insulting potential of any careless verbal communication between Self and Other. For example, in response to President Trump's two tweets from July 30, 2017 ("I am very disappointed in China. Our foolish past leaders have allowed them to make hundreds of billions of dollars a year in trade, yet …" and "they do NOTHING for us with North Korea, just talk. We will no longer allow this to continue. China could easily solve this problem!"), Chinese state media published a widely circulated editorial saying that "Trump is quite a personality, and he likes to tweet, however emotional venting cannot become the guidance for solving the nuclear issues on the Korean peninsula" (Westcott 2017). Obviously, social media diplomacy has opened many new opportunities for communication with both the public and diplomats. However, it comprises some risks including insulting ones when the writers discuss sensitive and difficult diplomatic issues.

Reflecting on Nick Miller's (2017) assumption that digital diplomacy could facilitate war between states, Manor points to arguments of both who believe it can lead to war and who think it reduces the risk of war (2017). Considering digital diplomacy as a powerful instrument, he, however, concludes that "The road to war remains a long one" (Manor 2017). But now we can see how social media can easily be a platform for "diplomatic schoolyard teasing".

> President Donald Trump is exchanging school yard taunts with North Korea's Kim Jong Un.
>
> In a response to North Korea calling Trump's speech in South Korea "reckless remarks by an old lunatic," Trump tweeted from Hanoi on Sunday morning: "Why would Kim Jong-un insult me by calling me 'old,' when I would NEVER call him 'short and fat?'"
>
> Trump goes on to say sarcastically, "Oh well, I try so hard to be his friend—and maybe someday that will happen!"
>
> TIME 2017

Obviously, this is not a typical diplomatic exchange. But it shows the tremendously extended "courtyard" of social media diplomacy.

The Range and Level of Symbolic Insult in Diplomacy

Scope of Symbolic Insult

Symbolic insult in diplomacy can be mild or severe, and the more affected the diplomatic actor's sense of Self is, the more painful the symbolic assault is. Actors can pay little attention or quickly forget minor symbolic offensive actions against them if they do not affect their dignity, integrity and social status. States can harshly disagree on some international issues and clearly see significant contradictions in their interests, but they may react to these differences with more tolerance than when others mock their identities, status, values or beliefs. One diplomatic actor can use a subtle form of symbolic offence on another actor so the latter may react to that act just with moderate negativity or even ignore it because a stronger reaction can put it in an awkward position or confront its strategic interests. Domestic actors may perceive symbolic offence or confrontation with external actors differently. For instance, on September 11, 2003, Russian President Vladimir Putin's op-ed was published in The New York Times where he, responding to President Barak Obama's reference to American exceptionalism, wrote that America is not exceptional (Putin 2013). President Obama didn't react, but Senator John McCain and then Speaker of the House of Representatives John Boehner considered Putin's the New York Times op-ed as an insult (Blake 2013).

Symbolic insult has a relational-normative dimension: a behavior which may not be considered as disgraceful, dishonorable and disrespectful among enemies, as it might be regarded as insulting among friends. That is why unfriendly countries may perceive spy scandals between them as more "normal" than countries that have allied relations. The same refers to the calling or labelling of other states: countries can overreact to an unpleasant remark of a representative of a friendly country while reacting more calmly to a similar statement by a representative of a less friendly country because in the existing relational-normative context, the first can affect their sense of Self to a greater extent. For example, in an interview with Geffrey Goldberg of the Atlantic magazine, President Obama gently rebuked some European allies, but the media especially reacted to his comments about the British Prime Minister David Cameron. Addressing the complete chaos and civil war in Libya, President Obama mentioned that Prime Minister Cameron soon stopped paying attention to that situation, becoming “distracted by a range of other things” (Goldberg 2016). As Gregory Katz remarked, “The British press on Friday accused President Barack Obama of launching an unprecedented verbal attack on British Prime Minister David Cameron in a magazine interview” (2016). Apparently, it would be hard to expect such a reaction from the British press if there were no “special relations” between the United States and the United Kingdom.

The discrepancy in seeing diplomatic normativity and ceremonial details by diplomatic actors may confuse or even humiliate one of them. One example is when Russian Foreign Minister Sergey Lavrov visited Mongolia on April 14, 2016 and “insulted his hosts by wearing blue jeans to a red carpet welcome” (Radchenko 2016). Sergey Radchenko referred to the Mongolian politician and political commentator B. Tsogtgerel who reported the incident as a snub, disrespect and insult. Radchenko stressed the importance of minor details, ceremony and protocol in diplomacy; however, “even then, one can never be sure one’s actions won’t be misconstrued as a hidden insult or a hideous plot” (2016). To avoid such incidents, diplomatic actors usually carefully arrange all the details of ceremonial events in advance.

We can speak about wider cross-cultural differences in understanding symbolic insult. The so-called Qaddafi shoe insult during the meeting between the former Libyan leader and British Prime Minister Tony Blair in 2004 is an example. “Arab commentators suggested that Gadaffi snubbed Blair by raising his shoe to reveal its sole during their meeting—a known insult in the Arab world” (Guardian 2004). Apparently, pointing the sole of a shoe towards an interlocutor is not considered as an insult in every country.

The same sort of act of one diplomatic actor on different actors can also be perceived differently by them. For example, it is often the case that states are pleased to receive foreign ambassadors who are fluent in their domestic languages, and many countries try to appoint ambassadors among those who know the language of the receiving state, or provide the newly appointed ambassadors with some linguistic training. That is a tradition and custom in diplomacy, which is useful in performing diplomatic duties abroad. However, sometimes countries send ambassadors abroad without the proper linguistic skills. Depending on cultural expectations and the status of the relationship, the receiving states can react to such an appointment differently. For some countries, that would be a minor disappointment, but for others, it may present a noticeable upset or even symbolically explicit disrespect.[22] Symbolic insult is a social construction where the cultural, perceptional and relational

22 France is known for its sensitivity about foreign diplomats’ knowledge of the French language. Here is a recent case: “U.S. Ambassador to France Jane D. Hartley, a major Obama

factors play a role. That is why diplomatic actors may design and use symbolic forms of offence on each other carefully by taking into consideration various political, social, cultural, emotional and other circumstances.

Symbolic Insult at High-Level Diplomacy

Heads of state and governments represent their countries internationally, and they symbolically embody the Self of their states and governments. Any symbolic harassment against them by other international actors is usually perceived by the domestic public indignantly. Therefore, top diplomats carefully try to avoid situations where they may lose face. Yet in diplomacy at the highest level, symbolically humiliating incidents may occur.

For example, in August 1942, the British Prime Minister Winston Churchill visited Moscow and met the Soviet leader Joseph Stalin in the Kremlin. Stalin insisted on the opening of a Second Front in Europe as soon as possible, but at that meeting Churchill informed him that this would not happen in 1942. As Stalin's interpreter Valentin Berejkov noted in his memoirs, the Soviet leader said slowly that the British should not be afraid of the Germans—they are not supermen. Then, Stalin asked Churchill why he is so afraid of them. According to Berejkov, Churchill considered these remarks offensive (1993). Stalin, apparently, played a diplomatic game of symbolic insult: in the context of the bargaining over the Second Front, he casually pounced on Churchill's Self whereas the latter had no doubt about the courage of the British and himself.

Churchill and Stalin had a complicated relationship, and they used both diplomatic sticks and carrots in their interactions. Another diplomatic incident happened in October 1943, when Churchill returned Stalin's unpleasant letter unopened, although the British Prime Minister knew the contents of this letter from its copy delivered before (Berthon and Potts 2007: 207–208). That episode took place in the context and as a part of disputes and negotiations between Stalin and Churchill over the Arctic convoy to deliver munitions and other war cargoes to the USSR during World War II.

Henry Kissinger mentioned a humiliating practice during a diplomatic summit in July 1958, when the Soviet leader Nikita Khruschev's visited China. On the second day of this visit, Chinese leader Mao Zedong received Khruschev "not in a ceremonial room but in his swimming pool. Khruschev, who could not swim, was obliged to wear water wings. The two statesmen conversed while swimming, with the interpreters following them up and down the side of the pool" (Kissinger 2011: 170). Kissinger himself cited William Taubman who

donor, has been mocked by the Parisian press for her poor French and for lack of influence in the country" (Palmeri 2017).

described how Khruschev later complained: "It was Mao's way of putting himself in an advantageous position. Well, I got sick of it … I crawled out, sat on the edge, and dangled my legs in the pool. Now I was on top and he was swimming below" (Kissinger 2011: 170). At that meeting, both leaders were involved in a game of tacit insulting.

Symbolic gestures play an important role in diplomacy, especially at the highest level, and there have been many cases of diplomatic breakthroughs with the help of goodwill gestures. However, symbolic gestures may also help diplomatic actors to humiliate or offend each other. The U.S. Secretary of State John Dulles's refusal to shake hands with Chinese Prime Minister Zhou Enlai at the Geneva Conference in 1954 is one of the well-known examples of symbolic insult in international diplomacy. As President Nixon wrote, "Zhou had been deeply offended when he extended his hand to John Foster Dulles at a public gathering and Dulles refused to shake it" (1980: 136). Dulles's humiliating gesture was not an expression of personal antipathy but rather a part of ongoing interactions and bargaining between the United States and China over several important issues. According to Kissinger (2011), Dulles's refusal to shake hands with Zhou Enlai reflected the United States' moral rejection and strategic design. From a negotiation perspective, that episode was part of a complicated and often tacit bargaining process between China and the United States over Taiwan, the recognition of the People's Republic of China and other challenging issues.

Raymond Cohen analyzed many cases of using nonverbal means within diplomatic community for tacit communication and bargaining. Some of them can be regarded as symbolic insult. For example, providing full protocol honors for governments-in-exile, or treating in exile leaders as heads of state (Cohen 1987: 144) is clearly asserting a symbolic insult on the governments and heads of state of the home country. But governments, for some reason, may informally soften the measures taken to put symbolic pressure on diplomats. Hervé Alphand gives an example, when after de Gaulle's veto of the British application to join the European Economic Community in 1963, the French Ambassador in Washington—"a well-linked and respected figure, found the White House closed to him", and President Kennedy, through his brother Robert, let the Ambassador "know that it would be better if he were not received for the moment" (Cohen 1987: 160). This episode shows that the diplomatic game of bargaining, as a part of strategic interactions, can be played at different levels, with varying degrees of openness, ambiguities of signaling and calculation of the diverse short-term and long-term factors.

The effects of symbolic insult often require symbolic healing. The so-called diplomacy of apology may be a part of symbolic reparation (Jones 2011; Cornut

2009). After the incident when Secretary of State Dulles refused to shake Chinese Prime Minister Zhou Enlai's hand in 1954, President Nixon was determined that his first act on arriving in China in 1972 would be to undo this act of omission. When Nixon descended from his plane, he stretched out his hand to Zhou Enlai, and the Chinese Premier took it. As Nixon pointed out, "it was more than a handshake. We both knew it was a turning point in history" (1980: 137). However, not all national humiliations can easily be compensated symbolically even over a long time. The historical memory sometimes only exacerbates the sense of damage, and politicians and elites can exploit past embarrassments for the development of their confrontational political narratives. As Alison Kaufman remarked, "Chinese elites today draw on the 'Century of Humiliation' (1839–1949) as a starting point for their views on how China should interact with other nations" (2010: 1). In this respect, Chinese elites are no different from elites in other countries: politicians, diplomats and other decision and opinion makers elsewhere widely practice narrative management and narrative bargaining for constructing and maintaining national identity and Self. In its turn, sense of Self becomes an important element of international strategic interactions, negotiations, bargaining and ontological security.

Tacit Bargaining and Symbolic Insult

Symbolism is a significant part of international negotiations and bargaining. In diplomacy, a negotiation venue, level and status of negotiators or delegations, their appearance, manners and body language, sitting arrangements and order of speeches, and so on may present a symbolic meaning and instrument of influence. So, negotiation symbolism can affect the mood and outcome of the negotiations. Diplomatic actors may use symbolism and symbolic insult in international negotiations and bargaining deliberately, unwittingly or spontaneously.

We distinguish international negotiation and bargaining: the first is a form of organized interaction between states or other international actors, while the second is not necessarily an organized process because often states bargain spontaneously or tacitly. Negotiation requires certain arrangements, and negotiation interaction in diplomacy usually takes place after some preparation or pre-negotiation. To organize a proper negotiation, actors need to set up an agenda and timeframes, define negotiators and their mandates, and clarify their interests and objectives. Sometimes parties can start negotiation with almost no preparation, but just their presence around a negotiation table points to some organized aspects of their interaction. By interacting with each other, however, diplomatic actors may not arrange all these practices but still bargain—albeit, more implicitly. Bargaining may also require some organizational input, though it can be done even without any preliminary arrangements.

Negotiation and bargaining are very close and overlapping terms, and there is no universally accepted understanding of their differences. Most scholars and practitioners associate bargaining with haggling and win/lose interactions, or tradeoffs which may lead to a gain of one party at the expense of the other. Through negotiation, however, although not always, diplomatic actors can find some common ground and can come to a mutually satisfactory agreement. In other words, bargaining is less controlled by norms and rules and a more tacit process where participants pursue only or primarily their own goals.

In his seminal book *The Strategy of Conflict*, Thomas Schelling distinguished and analyzed "explicit bargaining and the tacit kind in which adversaries watch and interpret each other's behavior, each aware that his own actions are being interpreted and anticipated, each acting with a view to the expectations that he creates" (1980: 21). Schelling used the term "tacit negotiation" as interchangeable with "tacit bargaining": both may lead to a "tacit agreement" or an agreement reached through partial or haphazard negotiation, or incomplete communication (1980: 75). "Focal point"—a solution arrived in such a situation—is a fundamental element of Schelling's theory of bargaining. Schelling, and then other scholars used the concept of focal point for the analysis of a wide range of bargaining situations, including diplomatic ones.

We approach international negotiations as organized interaction with its rules, procedures and other arrangements, while bargaining, in our opinion, may represent implicit and tacit interaction where the parties try to influence each other with less procedural measures and more ambiguity. In reality, most international negotiations incorporate elements of bargaining, and the bargaining process can comprise quite structured components. Some direct or indirect interactions between states or other international entities may not be seen as negotiation over particular issues though the actors could try to influence each other in order to achieve something they want. We may point to such strategic interactions as bargaining behavior, or strategic bargaining. The United States and Iran did not negotiate for a long time but constantly and indirectly they bargained over many issues. The same happens in relations between North Korea and the international community, or Israel and Hamas.

Tacit bargaining can take place between states and non-state actors, and it can use a variety of communication channels, including social media, organized public demonstrations, artistic performances and symbolically rich rituals and ceremonies. Culturally close nations can use commonly understood cultural codes and signals in bargaining (Faizullaev 2014 and 2017). Tacit bargaining between diplomatic actors is a never-ending process: when they interact directly or indirectly, they always bargain in one way or another.

Because of the mostly unarranged, implicit and flexible character of international bargaining, a hidden game of diplomacy with the use of symbolic offence is more present in bargaining between diplomatic actors than in explicit negotiations. Parties can apply manipulative strategies and tactics in arranged negotiations as well, but in comparison with implicit bargaining, explicit negotiation, especially when it has an agreed agenda and rules of procedure, provides fewer opportunities for the use of symbolic insult. For example, it is hard to imagine an inequality of flags of diplomatic representatives at an international conference in terms of their number and size. Nevertheless, even well-arranged diplomatic negotiations may provide many opportunities for implicit bargaining through manipulative interactions, sometimes by using insulting moves. Pressure, including a symbolic one, can affect negotiations. Parties concerned may appeal directly or indirectly to such delicate matters as national pride, historical heroes, the glorious past or the most sensitive issues for influencing the negotiation or bargaining outcome.

Bargaining may comprise various tacit instruments of advancing the bargainers' interests including a so-called bargaining chip. Usually a bargaining chip is not an obvious tool for making a deal or an agreement, so those who bargain or observe a bargaining interaction may not always detect its presence or be sure that someone has offered it. In other words, bargaining chips may appear ambiguously. This is the strength of a bargaining chip: it works seemingly casually, kind of unobtrusively, although it can be prepared thoroughly. For example, on December 3, 2016, U.S. President-elect Donald Trump had an unexpected telephone conversation with Taiwan's President Tsai Ing-wen, and Beijing with its "One China" policy took that as an insult (Chandran 2016). But because of the ambiguity of this diplomatic move, "strategists' views on the call with Tsai are mixed: It could be a calculated shift in U.S. foreign policy, a geopolitical game, or simply a rookie mistake" (Chandran 2016). However, many observers have seen this conversation as President-elect Trump's possible bargaining chip with China on some strategic issues of the U.S.-China relations. Unsurprisingly, some news headlines argued that the conversation was a bargaining chip, but others questioned the possibility: "Trump is Using Taiwan as a Bargaining Chip in Relations with China" (Jennings 2016), "Taiwan Fears Becoming Donald Trump's Bargaining Chip" (The Economist 2016), "Is Trump Using Taiwan as a Bargaining Chip with China?" (Schmitt 2016), "Is Taiwan a Bargaining-chip for Trump on China?" (Plett Usher 2016), and "Is Trump Using Taiwan as a China Bargaining Chip?" (Dyer 2016).

It is hard for diplomatic negotiators to avoid a symbolic frame of their meetings or a symbolic context for bilateral or multilateral relations. Symbolically meaningful framing, especially with the use of powerful metaphors, may become a tangible part of a symbolic game of influence, a means of the bargaining process. The Berlin Wall became an important symbol of the Cold War, and in 1987 in his West Berlin speech, U.S President Reagan "made the wall a metaphor for ideological and economic differences separating East and West" (Boyd 1987). Not surprisingly, the Soviet official press agency TASS reacted to the "Mr. Gorbachev, tear down this wall!" call abruptly by saying "Reagan delivered an openly provocative, war-mongering speech, in the spirit of the times of the Cold War" (Brammer 1987). That speech should be considered not only in the context of the Cold War and the Soviet-American confrontation but also within the framework of a series of meetings between President Reagan and the Soviet Leader Michael Gorbachev in the mid-1980s: the parties used various direct and indirect ways of negotiation and bargaining over many issues.

The Cold War itself became a symbol of global political confrontation, and the Cold War accusation turned to be an instrument of political pressure and international bargaining without a breakup of the relationship between the adversaries. In current hostile relations between Russia and the West, both sides continue to blame each other of fomenting a new Cold War. Here are some typical news headlines: "Russia, Germany trade Cold War accusations" (Baczynska 2015), "Russia's PM accuses West of rekindling Cold War" (Associated Press 2016), and "Polish President Duda says Russia fomenting New Cold War" (Sobczak and John 2016). The pursuit of the Cold War violates the idea of a post-Cold War era accepted by international public opinion, and the Cold War allegation appears to be part of a symbolic narration of an opponent's behavior in confrontational interactions and bargaining.

Roger Fisher, William Ury and Bruce Patton distinguished three categories of tricky bargaining tactics: deliberate deception, psychological warfare, and positional pressure (1991: 129–143). Psychological warfare is closer to a deliberative hurting of the opposite side's sense of Self. "Personal attack"—one of the methods of such a warfare with the use of verbal and nonverbal communication for making the opponent to feel uncomfortable—can manifest itself in comments on the counterparts' clothes or appearances, or attacking their status by making them wait for the offender, or interrupting negotiations to deal with other people, or implying their ignorance, or refusing to listen or making eye contact with them, or forcing them to repeat themselves (Fisher, Ury and Patton 1991: 135–136). Such tricky tactics can upset diplomatic actors, but because of the hidden nature of these kinds of manipulative actions, the harmed party may not know how to respond.

For achieving their political objectives, diplomatic actors may try to portray their opponents as unreliable and untrustworthy, and may ignore them or refuse to talk to them until those adversaries change their policy and behavior, and only start any kind of negotiation with heavy preconditions, or a lower the level of negotiators, a question of their values and intentions, a visit to ambiguous sites, an act of hosting the antagonists of the other side, etc. These practices can represent some features of the international bargaining processes—interactions between Self and Other with a concealed meaning.

Many observers viewed the Greek Prime Minister Alexis Tsipras' visit to Russia in April 2015 as a means of bargaining with the European Union at the height of the Greek debt crisis. "Tsipras plays the Russian Card", Deutsche Welle noted about this visit (2015). But even a few months before, Stratfor, a geopolitical intelligence company, pointed out that "During its first week in office, the Greek government confronted Germany and displayed its good ties with Russia. The moves are part of Athens' strategy for upcoming negotiations with lenders over debt relief" (2015). According to Dimitrios Trianaphyllou, the European Union had a reason to be concerned over relations between Greece and Russia: the Greece Prime Minister Alexis Tsipras' visit to Moscow brought to the spotlight "fears that Greece may be breaking ranks with its allies and partners" (2015). As for Emmanuel Karagiannis, the main reason behind the media and huge public attention to this visit "is that Greece has been constantly suspected of being a Trojan Horse for Russian interests in the Old Continent" (2015). In short, many observers saw that visit as a part of a global bargaining process and an action containing a symbolic threat to the EU's sense of Self.

When Agriculture Minister of Poland Marek Sawicki called on Russian President Vladimir Putin to halt the destruction of Polish food imports confiscated at the Russian border by "referring to the 1930s hunger in Ukraine which was deliberately caused on Stalin's orders and involved destruction of grain hidden by farmers from the authorities" (Radio Poland 2015), the Russian Embassy in Warsaw "called statements of the minister offensive and irrelevant" (Glavnoe 2015). This exchange can be analyzed not only in the context of the destruction of the imported products but in the wider context of the Polish-Russian relationship, and mutual influence and bargaining between Russia and the European Union over many issues as well as symbolic interaction of Russia's and Poland's Selves.

Negotiators may have zones of their symbolic comfort and discomfort, and that may exert pressure on themselves. For example, it is socially expected to see a top level diplomatic negotiator from a powerful country with certain symbolic attributes of power and prestige, including an entourage, a limousine and a visible place at the negotiation table. Any failure of meeting those social expectations may adversely affect the power, possibilities and self-regard of such a negotiator.

Face Diplomacy and Symbolic Insult

As I already pointed out, when Other challenges the very identity and integrity of Self, its core values and essential norms and means of existence, the Self may perceive this as an existential threat and become very sensitive to everything that approves or threatens its sense of Self. In such a challenging situation, issues of dignity, honor, respect, and status as well as humiliation, embarrassment and shame acquire a greater significance for Self, its identity, oneness, security and existence.

For the diplomatic actor, "social virtues" (recognition, status, respect, honor, dignity, face and tact) and self-regard are important not just in themselves but for the fulfilment of the actor's political, moral, social and legal imperatives. Above we discussed some of these factors. Here I would like to elaborate on the role of "face" and "face-work" in international diplomacy and their relations with diplomatic insults. The concept of face is closely linked with the concepts of image, appearance, representation and impression. Diplomats appear as the face of their nation on the international stage, and their actual appearance plays a role in that process. How diplomats look, what kind of impression they make—these are not secondary issues in diplomacy. The image of a diplomat is a part of a national image, and image-making is an essential function of diplomacy. Face-saving corresponds to the essence of diplomacy.

We can approach "face" as a sense of Self exposed publicly. Erving Goffman's concepts of face and face-work provide a useful theoretical framework for analyzing relations between the sense of Self and the management of the actor's public image. Defining face as "an image of self delineated in terms of approved social attributes" (1967: 5), Goffman studied the so-called face-work—"the actions taken by a person to make whatever he is doing consistent with face" (1967: 12). Goffman pointed to some similarities between face-work and diplomacy by saying that the capacity of face-work "is sometimes called tact, savoir-faire, diplomacy, or social skill" (1967: 13). In international diplomacy, face-work can pinpoint a group of practices directed to building the diplomatic actor's positive self-image or self-concept and also its attempt to protect a positive sense of Self.

In diplomacy, management of face or face-work can be considered both figuratively and literally. In a figurative sense, that is related to a nation's face. But face-work takes place also literally at the individual level. For example, often diplomats, when they are in a professional setting or public space, try to keep serious faces, and that is a manifestation of the "properness" of their faces. When diplomacy is considered as a serious business, improper face expression appears as a threat to the diplomatic social status and the actor's sense of Self.

Adler-Nissen devoted a special attention to impression management and face-work in diplomacy (2012). Based on Erving Goffman's dramaturgical model (Goffman 1959) and his concept of face-work (Goffman 1967), this paper argues that diplomacy can be seen as national face-work, and "diplomatic interaction order centred around impression management, face-work and a strong focus on avoidance of embarrassment" (Adler-Nissen 2012: 7). By pointing to the importance of maintaining face in diplomacy, Adler-Nissen stressed the inevitable relations between diplomatic social norms, face-work and embarrassment as well as the anticipation of embarrassment. Thus, diplomatic protocol and tact strongly affect face-work and management of embarrassment in diplomacy. "Playing equals demands tact and effort from both sides and a lot of management of embarrassment" (Adler-Nissen 2012: 11). However, as Adler-Nissen remarked, when diplomats improvise and engage in strategic face-work, sometimes they violate norms. That can create the embarrassing situation where diplomats may lose face. In such a situation, tact can be employed to treat the embarrassment (Adler-Nissen 2012: 21). Apparently, tact can also be employed to avoid the embarrassment and protect the actor's sense of Self.

Adler-Nissen pointed to important aspects of diplomatic face-work in relations with avoiding and managing embarrassment, particularly when one of the interacting sides violates norms and acts inappropriately. In this paper, we pay attention to diplomatic face-work in relations with a calculated subtle insult. Such an effort can be seen as a part of face-saving diplomacy, or face diplomacy—diplomatic face-work that takes place when an engagement between Self and Other affects the diplomatic actor's public image and social status.[23]

Face diplomacy can appear as a part of policy of prestige and status, or be practiced alone in usual diplomatic encounters. Face diplomacy as a form of international face-work points to interaction between Self and Other, especially symbolic and strategic interaction with an image related consequence. The

---

23 Holmes (2013) also used the concept of face in studying diplomacy. By approaching personal diplomacy as the practice of face-to-face diplomacy, he offered a "mirror neurons" approach to interpersonal interaction in diplomacy. While Holmes uses some findings of neuroscience and political psychology, we advance here more sociological understanding the role of face in diplomacy in the spirit of Goffman's works.

important part of the face-work, in the context of this paper, is that it "serves to counteract 'incidents'—that is, events whose effective symbolic implications threaten face" (Goffman 1967: 12). Face diplomacy can be conducted to avoid national embarrassment, insult and humiliation, to protect collective Self from symbolic insult committed by Other, or as retaliation from the humiliated side. In a conflict environment, diplomatic face-work also appears as a behavior for protecting the nation's ontological security. Sometimes threats to face "must be resisted by war" (O'Neil 2001: 139), but often that requires more delicate face diplomacy. Diplomatic face-work is closely connected with a narrative work—a political storytelling: politicians and diplomats who found themselves in an awkward situation, may try to explain the embarrassed/insulted/humiliated happening in their own way.

Face diplomacy is particularly relevant in relationships between strategic rivals. Propaganda and/or public diplomacy that accompany confrontational relationships between countries, can be directed not just towards the other party, but also towards building a collective sense of self-affirmation and saving face, i.e. it may be essentially inward-oriented.

Countries commonly resort to symbolic insult and face diplomacy when military confrontation between them carries a threat of mutual destruction. As an example, we can take the Soviet-American and then Russian-U.S. confrontational relations, where the sense of honor and national pride on the one hand, and humiliation, insult and embarrassment, on the other, played an essential role. For a long time, honor was, and remains, the main motive of Russia's relations with the West (Tsygankov 2012). Symbolism and symbolic rivalry is a part of Russia's relentless quest for equal status with the West (Neumann and Pouliot 2011). In such a context, Self may see the success of the rival Other as a symbol of humiliation, and diplomacy may impose some symbolic insult on the opponent.

For example, on October 4, 1957, the Soviet Union launched Sputnik, the first artificial Earth satellite. Sputnik "essentially forced the United States to place a new national priority on research science, which led to the development of microelectronics—the technology used in today's laptop, personal, and handheld computers" (Dickson 2001, 4). The success of the Sputnik operation caused "a sudden crisis of confidence in American technology, values, politics, and the military" (Dickson 2001: 4), and "national insecurity, wounded national pride, infighting, political grandstanding, clandestine plots, and ruthless media frenzy were but a few of the things the United States had to overcome to bounce back from the blow dealt to the nation by Sputnik" (Dickson 2001: 7). On November 3, 1957, the Soviet Union launched a second Sputnik satellite, and in two months, on December 6, the first American satellite—Vanguard

3TV—exploded during takeoff, adding more embarrassment to the nation's mood. On the same day, according to Paul Dickson, the Soviet delegation to the United Nations offered financial aid to the United States "as part of a program of technical assistance to backward nations", and as such, "America's humiliation was complete" (Dickson 2001: 159).

Face diplomacy is a delicate social practice, and everything that surrounds face-to-face summit meetings and especially their nonverbal aspects—handshakes, facial expressions, the tone of the speeches, posture, etc. can help to better understand this phenomenon. One of the face related elements of summit diplomacy is the issue of who initiated whom. The following case illustrates such a sensitive moment pertaining to the conflicting relationship between Self and Other. After two years of absence of official meetings between Russian President Vladimir Putin and the United States President Barak Obama due to the deterioration of Russian-American relations, the leaders agreed to meet on September 28, 2015, in New York during the United Nations General Assembly. The importance of this meeting was evident but both sides, tying to rise to the occasion, publicly denied the proposal of the summit. As Peter Baker (2015) remarked, "the jockeying over who invited whom underscored the delicacy of the meeting at a time of great tension between the United States and Russia over the conflicts in Ukraine and Syria".

The Russian-American social game of diplomatic slapping has continued around the expected meeting between President Vladimir Putin and President Donald Trump during the Asia-Pacific Economic Cooperation (APEC) summit in Vietnam in November 2017. The Kremlin announced that there will be such a meeting but the White House said that no meeting was scheduled (Meyer and Arkhipov 2017). Nevertheless, in Russia there were big expectations about it. In fact, the Presidents had just brief informal encounters but no formal meeting. In Russia, some observers and commentators considered this as a frustrating or even humiliating incident. "Putin later told reporters that the failure to meet was due to 'certain protocol formalities which our teams, unfortunately, failed to coordinate,' and that officials 'will be disciplined for that'" (Meyer and Arkhipov 2017). Russian President also admitted that the absence of the separate meeting "showed that relations between Russia and the United States had not yet overcome their state of crisis" (Sputnik 2017 a). Putin's press secretary noted, that the American side tried to negotiate a separate bilateral meeting between the two Presidents but suggested a time and place that suited only them (RIA Novosti 2017). Some Russian politicians and commentators blamed anti-Russian political forces in the United States for the absence of the expected meeting. "Russian lawmakers and analysts bemoaned U.S. President Donald Trump's failure to hold a formal meeting with Kremlin counterpart

Vladimir Putin at the APEC summit in Vietnam, as state media sought to put a brave face on the perceived snub" (Meyer and Arkhipov 2017). The Kremlin face-work was supported by the Russian state media. "The official government daily, Rossiyskaya Gazeta, led its front page Monday with a photograph of Trump and Putin talking as they walked during the summit with the headline: 'Road Map. War with Terrorism to Continue. But That's Not Enough.' Still, the newspaper noted that the two presidents spoke briefly 'at least three times'" (Meyer and Arkhipov 2017). "Big Men Need a Few Words: Trump-Putin 'Talk' Captured on VIDEO in Vietnam", was a headline of the article in Sputnik news agency's website, controlled by the Russian Government (Sputnik 2017 a). A public sense of Self, fueled public by anticipations may undergo damage if the expectations are not met. In such cases, sometimes even retroactively, face diplomacy aims to mitigate the effects.

The Self of a diplomatic actor is formed in interaction with Other, and communication and meetings with others are crucial for the actor's self-perception and their perception by the public. Therefore, it is quite unpleasant for the Self when the significant Other refuses, especially in public, to attend a requested meeting. That happened in October 2015, when the United States refused to receive a high-level delegation from Russia headed by Prime Minister Dmitry Medvedev. In his press briefing, the White House Press Secretary Josh Earnest (2015) explained the reason for this refusal by saying that the United States "would welcome a constructive Russian contribution that's integrated with the international effort against ISIL that's currently underway", "but Russia has a different plan". The Russian President and Prime Minister reacted very negatively to this rejection from the United States (Litvinova 2015). So, face diplomacy can be an arena for both taking a symbolic jab at the opponent and protecting Self from the symbolic threat of Other.

In high-level diplomacy, both refusals to offer an invitation for a meeting and to accept an invitation, create an awkward situation and may affect national pride. The absence of Russia at the Nuclear Security Summit in 2016, held in Washington, DC was seen by many observers as another manifestation of the complications in Russian-American relations. "Putin snubs Obama, skips D.C. nuclear summit amid Islamic State fears", was a distinctive headline of an article in The Washington Times (Boyer 2016). The issuing of invitations and meetings may become part of the social game of international diplomacy around diplomatic actors' Selves. In diplomatic practice, national interest, values, relationships and rights are closely intertwined with national honor and face.

Confrontation between major nuclear powers at a symbolic level appears as an element of their total opposition at various levels and with many components: political, economic, military, moral, social, narrative, and so on. Symbolic insult can manifest all these aspects of hostility. But symbolic clash, affecting the actors' Selves, can instigate other elements of resentment, especially when it happens publicly and disgraces both sides. That is the danger of symbolic affront. However, a subtle symbolic insult that gives the possibility for face-work can provide Self and Other the opportunity to negotiate and find some balance between the interests and relationships of the involved parties. Face diplomacy is a diplomacy that may allow the parties to save their faces in public.[24]

Apparently, any face diplomacy needs to be considered in a wide context with the consideration of global political, bilateral and cultural factors. It is also important to pay attention to the so-called international pecking orders which describe "the informal hierarchies of standing that pervade multilateral organizations such as the UN" (Pouliot 2016: 2). Viewing the sovereign equality of the United Nations member states as a misperception, Jonathan Renshon considered hierarchy but not equality as the fundamental ordering principle of international politics (2017: 1). According to Pouliot, "multilateral diplomacy produces inequality", and "that international pecking orders emerge out of the multilateral diplomatic process itself" (2016: 2). This is because diplomatic practices in a multilateral setting—socially organized ways of doing things—generate social stratification, inequality and diplomatic sense of place (Pouliot 2016: 2–3). An individual diplomat may be a part of this pecking order and act in accordance with the requirements of this order. However, external observers, especially those who are affected by the collective sense of Self, may perceive such an adaptability of a diplomat as a threat to national pride and condemn it. In other words, a diplomatic sense of place and public sense of self-regard may not always coincide. The discrepancy between the diplomatic and public view of the international pecking order may comprise a humiliating risk. So, face diplomacy has both international and domestic dimensions.

Analyzing the development of the modern public diplomacy, Jan Melissen noted, that due to broadened opportunities of access to information, citizens

24 The ambiguity of diplomatic signaling and symbolic gestures in diplomacy can also be instrumental in face saving. That happened, for example, in 2001 in the Hainan Island incident between China and the United States over a mid-air collision of a U.S. reconnaissance aircraft and Chinese fighter jet and landing the American surveillance plane on Hainan Island and the death of a Chinese pilot: China demanded an official apology, and the United States offered an ambiguous letter of regret and sorrow. Such a careful symbolic gesture allowed both sides to save their faces and overcome a diplomatic deadlock (Zhang 2001; Cornut 2011).

turned "into independent observers as well as assertive participants in international politics" (2005: 24). In such a situation, foreign ministries and diplomats forced to "increasingly take into account the concerns of ordinary people", and that poses "a formidable challenge for diplomatic practitioners who feel more comfortable operating within their own professional circle" (Melissen 2005: 24). By observing and affecting international politics and diplomacy, people also push diplomats and other representatives of the state in international public arena to engage with image making activities and raise their face-work to a new level.

Public opinion, media and social media have a big impact on modern diplomacy. Different social groups and individuals now have a greater opportunity to express not only their rational opinions but also emotions about international politics and diplomatic activities. This increases the risk of a mismatch between the diplomats' and the public's sense of Self in relations with other countries and their representatives. The widened opportunities for ordinary people to observe diplomatic events, the enhanced influence of the public on diplomacy and high sensitivity of public opinion and the media to diplomatic insults and humiliations are playing a role in the current—enlarged—visibility of symbolic insults in diplomacy. This also puts an additional burden on face diplomacy.

Referring to the agent-structure discourse in international relations theory (Wendt 1987), we may see the audience or observers as a part of international/diplomatic structure where diplomats (agents) act and interact. In the modern world, where the public increasingly influences the characteristics of the international/diplomatic environment, and observers become a kind of international/diplomatic actors, diplomats as agents also gain new opportunities—with the use of media, Internet and social media that multiply the channels of communication—to shape the international structure. In other world, we see the growing interdependence of diplomatic actors and public observers.

Handshake Diplomacy and Symbolic Insult

Handshake Diplomacy

Body language is an important part of diplomatic communication, and it provides a much-needed flexibility and constructive ambiguity in signaling (Morgenthau 1993; Cohen 1987; Jönsson and Aggestam 1999). Diplomatic body language may include military parades or redeployment of warships, ceremonies and rituals, the use of flags and other national symbols, tone of written and oral messages, diplomatic premises, cars, dresses and entourages, facial expression and gestures of individual diplomats. Body language, especially gestures, can be a source of both symbolic kindness and insult in diplomacy. "Gestures constitute a considerable part of the "vocabulary" of abuse. Like verbal vehicles, gestures are symbolic actions designated as expressions of put-downs, affront, and ridicule" (Conley 2010: 22). Gestures such as voting at a diplomatic conference or the UN Security Council meeting can be interpreted as a snub or a moment of pride by a concerned country.

A considerable portion of modern diplomacy at a high level takes place in public, under the observation of television and photo journalists and viewers. As Cohen remarked, public behavior cannot be permitted the luxury of spontaneity, so "politics requires that it be calculated and controlled" (1987: 89). However, the theatrical dimension and loss of spontaneity of political behavior "has strengthened rather than weakened the communicatory value of 'body language'": "what gestures have lost in sincerity, they have gained in informativeness" (Cohen 1987: 90). Apparently, calculated gestures and other elements of body language can be used for face-work, protection of the sense of Self and debasing the opponent.

In this part of the paper I focus on non-verbal aspects of greetings in diplomacy, or the diplomacy of handshakes. In fact, diplomacy itself is often associated with the image of a handshake. Indeed, diplomacy may start with a handshake and the absence of a handshake can indicate a lack of diplomacy and goodwill. A handshake is a contact, a tangible one. In public, it becomes an essential part of social acceptance, an instrument of honoring and face-work. Although a handshake is not practiced in all cultures, it is more or less universally adopted as an international salutation, and seen as a symbolic form of a basic regard (Cohen 1987: 91). Because of the social symbolism of a handshake, that gesture plays such a prominent role in diplomacy. However, a handshake can be not only friendly, respectful and rewarding but also unfriendly, disrespectful and insulting. A handshake can send ambiguous signals too. Diplomats may employ a handshake for demonstrating honor and respect as well as signaling displeasure, indifference, neglect and disregard. Diplomacy can use "the calculated snub—the demonstrative refusal to shake hands when the hand is proffered" (Cohen 1987: 93). The duration of the handshake is also relevant: "a brief clasp of the hands clearly lacks warmth, especially if the occasion calls for something more emphatic", and "the long, drawn-out handshake is theatrically cordial" (Cohen 1987: 94–95). Because of the semantic richness of the diplomatic handshake, this gesture attracts considerable interest from journalists and the public.

The public handshake of countries' representatives can present a message about the status of bilateral relations and the parties' attitudes and intentions.

However, as with any other type of body language, a handshake is not always controlled completely by the individual, and its uncontrolled elements also convey a message. For diplomats, their handshake affects their public face, so it is a meaningful part of their interactions. The collective sense of Self related to diplomatic behavior is very sensitive to all aspects of public handshakes. Handshake diplomacy is sensitive for such questions as with whom, when and how does the representative of a country greet, and does the other side demonstrate proper respect? A mutually respectful handshake with a decent Other positively affects the collective sense of Self, and a handshake with a controversial figure can cause resentment. When President of the United States, Barack Obama friendly shook hands with Venezuelan President Hugo Chávez during the Fifth Summit of the Americas in Trinidad and Tobago on April 17, 2009, some prominent members of the Republican party criticized this gesture as "irresponsible" and "not helpful" (Kaplan 2009). Obama defended his greeting, saying that "the United States, with its overwhelming military superiority and need to improve its global image, could afford to extend such diplomatic 'courtesy'" (Nicholas 2009). So, a handshake with a foreign leader can appear as a meaningful instrument of both international and domestic politics.

There are numerous publications on this matter, especially by journalists who are keen to read and interpret handshake diplomacy and its nuances. This is because a handshake is a visible, symbolic and meaningful diplomatic gesture. Here we analyze the case of handshake diplomacy between the U.S. President Donald Trump and President of France Emmanuel Macron on the 25th and 26th May, 2017. The handshakes between the two presidents were widely discussed internationally.

Of course, any handshake between politicians should be considered not just as an act of situational nonverbal communication between important individuals but also analyzed in the context of wider political and bilateral relationships, taking into consideration each party's imperatives. But because of the distinctiveness of President Trump's handshakes, his handshake diplomacy has attracted a large interest.[25] As Elizabeth Preza put it, "perhaps no hands in history have been covered as extensively as Donald Trump's" (2017). This represents not just an interest in an individual's handshake but is apparently a

25 According to Meg Wagner, "Trump's handshakes have become signature moments in his interactions with world leaders. While Japanese Prime Minister Shinzo Abe visited the White House in February, Trump shook his hand for 19 seconds, even patting it several times and pulling it closer. A month later, Trump apparently declined to shake German Chancellor Angela Merkel's hand during an Oval Office meeting, though he shook it other times in her visit to Washington" (2017).

willingness to understand the motives and intentions of a powerful politician and the country he represents through his expressive handshaking behavior. President Trump's handshake is an interesting phenomenon to study from the perspective of diplomatic symbolic insult.

President Trump's Unique Handshake Power Game

Before analyzing the meeting between President Trump and President Macron, let's highlight some views about Donald Trump's handshake. This handshake has attracted huge media and social media interest. "The Trump handshake has become the most unique greeting in all of politics," and "among social media spectators, anticipating what sort of handshake President Trump will deploy in his public interactions has become something of a sport" (Rogers 2017). Many observers recognize the uniqueness of his handshake and its importance as a political gesture. "US President Donald Trump is renowned for his unusual handshakes with world leaders" (ABC News 2017), and "if you want to better understand Donald Trump—his presidency, his approach personal diplomacy, even his psyche—simply follow his hands" (Stein 2017). In any case, President Trump's handshake has become a visible and extensively discussed part of his diplomatic activities. Apparently, Trump's handshake diplomacy can be considered in the context of his extreme attention to symbolism, status, respect and personal prestige (Wolf 2017).

Donald Trump's handshake has been portrayed as an "alpha handshake" (Preza 2017), "power handshake" (Shephard 2017), "white-knuckle handshake" (Barnes 2017; Cillizza 2017), "the aggressive" and "yank and pull handshake" (Jain 2017), "'pull' and forceful style of handshake" (Iovine 2017), a "yankshake", "clasp and yank", "macho arm-yank handshake thing" (Blagburn 2017), and "a friendly death grip" (Rogers 2017). Most observers perceive this handshake as a kind of power game, or "the opening salvo in a battle for supremacy" (The Conversation 2017). For psychologist Florin Dolcos, "this could be Trump's way of asserting dominance, and that he may even practice these handshakes" (Iovine 2017), and for body language expert Darren Stanton "it's all about the assertion of power and control" (Hosie 2017). In diplomacy, if one side tries to assert dominance and supremacy, we may expect that the other side is in a difficult situation.

Here are some essential elements of Donald Trump's handshake. He "uses handshakes as a weapon in his games of one-upmanship": "he pulls them forwards into his personal space, unbalancing them, and putting them at an immediate disadvantage" (The Conversation 2017). Rachel Hosie (2017) noted that "the President has a propensity to yank the hand of his unsuspecting victim towards him—sometimes multiple times—vigorously jerk the hand up and down, and often pat it a couple of times with his other hand". That means any foreign leader who is going to greet the American President, may be in a competitive situation and should be prepared in order to not be embarrassed.

> Senior politicians expecting routine and formulaic handshakes have been knocked off guard by Trump's unpredictable behaviour. They find themselves yanked into his personal space, where it is difficult or impossible for them to make eye contact, or to talk coherently without looking away. This gives Trump an advantage in the game of micro-politics.
>
> His handshakes are clearly all about status rather than solidarity. From a psychological perspective, they are arguably self-serving and egocentric, and demonstrate that, as in many aspects of life, the most important thing to Donald Trump is Donald Trump himself.
>
> THE CONVERSATION 2017

In short, Donald Trump's handshake behavior is seen by many observers as a form of political and personal contest, as his attempt to gain power and status. Chris Cillizza (2017) remarked that "Trump seems to view the handshake as a sort of battle of wills and a battle for power all wrapped into one". According to Francis Blagburn (2017), "for Donald Trump, a handshake is a thumb war: a raging battle into which all four of his fingers will inevitably become embroiled". Because of some association of such a handshake with fight and Donald Trump's technique, "one martial arts school has even come up with advice on how to defend it" (The Conversation 2017). They offered a tutorial on how to defend against President Trump's handshakes when he pulls forcefully on the hand he's shaking (Firozi 2017).

In such a competitive situation, a greeted person—especially if he or she is a statesman, a senior diplomat or another public figure—can face a risk of unbalancing and downgrading his or her social status, and that means being embarrassed or humiliated. For a foreign leader, this might become a symbolic game of saving face, or part of face diplomacy.

President Trump and President Macron: First Meeting and Handshake Diplomacy

For both the United States and France, their relationship with each other represents great significance. This relationship was not always easy but historically has had constant importance. Therefore the first meeting between a relatively new U.S. President Donald Trump and just recently elected President of France Emmanuel Macron—with their policy differences, particularly on climate issues, immigration, the roles of NATO and the European Union—

attracted a large interest. The more liberal and global political philosophy of the French President versus the "America First" approach of the U.S. President as well as their different personal styles, also contributed to the international and media focus on this meeting.

President Trump and President Macron met in Brussels for first time on May 25, 2017. The first meeting of the two powerful leaders was a symbolic event in itself. They greeted each other with "a super-strong competitive handshake" (Gopnik 2017). We can assume that Emmanuel Macron did his homework on shaking hands with Donald Trump. "Each man gripped the other's hand so firmly that their knuckles turned white and their jaws seemed to clench" (BBC News 2017 a). The shaking process "lasted over 5.2 seconds and included an unsuccessful attempt by Trump at one point to release himself from his counterpart's grasp" (Kelsey 2017). Many videos and photos of this interaction and commentaries appeared in the media and social media. Some observers described this event as a thrilling sporting competition. Elena Cresci (2017) from the Guardian noted that "for a brief moment it seemed neither man wanted to give up, which would have made everything even more awkward, but in the end Trump relented and loosened his fingers". According to the Reuters (2017 b) observation, "images from the photo session at the U.S. ambassador's residence in Brussels showed Trump finally giving up, his fingers loosened while Macron is still holding on tightly". Here are the remarks of Tom Porter from Newsweek about Emmanuel Macron's view of this handshake:

> France's new president Emmanuel Macron described a white-knuckle handshake in which he refused to relinquish his grip on U.S. president Donald Trump's hand as "not innocent."
>
> In an interview with the Journal du Dimanche Sunday, the French leader said his interaction with the American head of state was "a moment of truth."
>
> "My handshake with him was not innocent. We need to show that we won't make small concessions, even symbolic ones, while not overhyping things either," Macron said.
>
> "Donald Trump, the Turkish president or the Russian president believe in the logic of the trial of strength, which doesn't bother me. I don't believe in the diplomacy of public invective, but in my bilateral dialogues, I don't let anything pass, that is how we are respected," he said.
>
> PORTER 2017

As we can see, President Macron was well-prepared for the diplomacy of public invective—a competitive public handshake with President Trump. Loosing this challenging game could weaken his public image. Emmanuel Macron received many remarks praising his victorious handshake battle from his supporters on social media. The media and public saw this handshake interaction as an important test for the new French President's character and will, and his successful standing against Donald Trump's powerful handshake was perceived as a sign of his global leadership potential. The handshake between the two presidents symbolized many significant aspects of bilateral relations. We can also see this nonverbal interaction as an element of reestablishing (from the French President's side) or effort of proving (from the American President's side) an existing international pecking order. It was both politically and personally important for both sides, especially for President Macron, to show the strength. However, "clear victory" also comprised some risk: it could damage interpersonal relations and humiliate the other side. So, the symbolic game of Self/Other manifested in handshake may be even more complicated than just demonstrating the strength and standing.

The Trump-Macron symbolic power game did not finish with their first handshake. "Later in the day, there was a rematch between the two foes" (Cresci 2017). This time events took place around the symbolism of "who would greet whom first".

> The symbolic face-off continued later in the day at a NATO summit, as Macron approached a group of other leaders and made Trump wait, firstly exchanging greetings with Merkel, the head of the Western military bloc, and others.
>
> When Trump finally seized Macron's hand, he pulled it so hard that the French president had to use his other arm to set himself free, their second awkward moment that was caught on cameras and went viral in just one day.
>
> REUTERS 2017 B

So, the French President's attempt to reestablish a NATO pecking order by not greeting President Trump first was met by the American President's more successful handshake rematch. Sam Stein (2017) pointed out that "as Macron approached Trump and other world leaders at the opening of NATO's new headquarters in Brussels last week, the U.S. president offered several nonverbal cues indicating his desire to re-establish the global pecking order" (Stein 2017). Some reporters saw Macron's behavior as snubbing Trump. Joe Barnes (2017) wrote that the American President "offered one of his trademark 'white-knuckle' handshakes to Emmanuel Macron after the French president appeared to snub the American for Angela Merkel". The Telegraph provided the following account of this "apparent snub":

> Emmanuel Macron swerves to avoid Donald Trump and embrace German chancellor Angela Merkel instead, in a video that has emerged of the apparent snub in Brussels.
>
> The newly elected French President tweeted the video of himself walking up the red carpet towards the group of Nato leaders, seemingly headed straight towards the US President.
>
> But at the last second Mr Macron ducks to the right and shares a warm embrace with Mrs Merkel, leaving Mr Trump to lower his hands awkwardly back down to his sides.
>
> Mr Macron then proceeds to greet other leaders including Mr Trump, who grabs his French counterpart's hand with a characteristic pumping action.
>
> FOREIGN STAFF OF THE TELEGRAPH 2017

However, not everybody saw this episode as a calculated snub or slap. "It's unclear whether the possible snub was deliberate. But it came amid a summit in which Trump took aim at NATO's European allies for 'not paying what they should be paying'", remarked Lee Moran (2017). According to Alis Folley (2017), "it is unclear as to whether or not Macron's swerve was deliberate". However, Folley (2017) added: "Macron's post has since gone viral, with many of his followers seeming to appreciate his apparent snub towards Trump". Subtle insult in diplomacy, or diplomatic slap/snub—because of its ambiguity—is difficult to detect and decode definitively. Nevertheless, it delivers a message.

Donald Trump and Emmanuel Macron have entered the subtle game of nonverbal rope pulling. So far they are successfully balancing their political and relationship imperatives: on the one hand, they defend and promote their political interests, and on the other, keep decent relationships. After these encounters in Brussels, President Macron invited President Trump and his wife to Paris for the Bastille Day celebrations as guests of honor. Apparently, they have developed a good relationship, and several times praised each other. However, their handshake game continued in Paris. On July 14, 2017, the two presidents "held on to each other as they walked. Mr Trump at one point pulled the smaller Mr Macron off balance and held fast as they approached their wives" (ABC News 2017 b). The episode lasted around 30 seconds, and "it was a new and prolonged take on their famous knuckle-whitening handshake of late May in Brussels" (Chappell 2017).

The Trump-Macron handshake diplomacy is affected by many factors including political and diplomatic, status and face, as well as the personalities of the two men. Perhaps we may expect different dynamics from their handshake diplomacy depending on all the potentially significant factors involved. So far it has been on the verge of embarrassing the Other by keeping the sense of strong Self. But when the public is so involved in such a game, there exists a risk to tread into the territory of insult/humiliation.

Conclusion

Diplomacy has a civilizing mission, and international law, universal human values and diplomatic culture provide norms and framework for civilized conduct and dialogue between and among nations. The word "diplomacy" has such synonyms or properties as delicacy, subtlety, tact, savoir-faire, finesse, artfulness, grace, civility, courtesy and discretion. And the word "insult" bordered with such terms as offence, affront, outrage, abuse, slap, snub, disgrace, disrespect and indignity. So, these two words—"diplomacy" and "insult"—imply quite opposite meanings, and the expression "diplomatic insult" appears to be nonsensical, or at least paradoxical. Like "diplomacy without being diplomatic", or "insult without insulting".

How can diplomacy, with its care about peace and relationships, coexist with insult that can destroy peace and relations? Why does symbolic insult take place in diplomacy? And why sometimes diplomats and other state representatives deliberately commit insult, even if they know that this can cause a conflict and lead to the deterioration of relations? The point is that diplomatic activities are inseparable from international politics based on the interests of diplomatic actors, and these interests may not coincide. But apart from interest-based imperatives, the behavior of diplomatic actors can be instigated by their value-based, relationship-based and right-based imperatives. This paper shows that in diplomacy, Self can commit a concealed symbolic insult against Other when it wants to promote its interests on the one hand, while on the other, it wishes to keep some normative relationships with the latter. In order to do so, diplomatic actors can try to weaken the opponent's sense of Self but not totally destroy it. In other words, symbolic insult in diplomacy is a form of both strategic and emotional "stroke", or "slap in the face" undertaken by the diplomatic actor while defending its interests in dealing with the adversary. But such an action is constrained by the need to keep relationship with the other party.

Diplomacy is considered to be an activity, which, in contrast to war, uses peaceful and civilized means to fulfil its noble mission. Indeed, diplomacy plays an indispensable role in international conflict resolution and achieving understanding among nations. However, diplomats can also play, using the expression of Michael Gordon and Gardiner Harris, "a subtle game of diplomatic poker" (2015). Sometimes they do not pay much attention to such a game because that is already in their habitus, and they see their main task as defending and promoting the interests, values, rights and relationships of the countries they represent or the wider international community, and they try to use their diplomatic skills for achieving their objectives. But this game transforms into an intangible or symbolic insult when it hurts the opponent's sense of Self—a fundamental aspect of the actor's identity, social being and ontological security.

Self is a product of social interactions, and symbolic insult in diplomacy comes up as a social phenomenon with political content: it occurs in a normative environment, relates to cultural codes, depends on social perception and practices, and affects the relationship between diplomatic actors, their international status, dignity, self-regard and well-being—the whole selfhood.

Self-affirmation through the fulfilment of the actor's political, moral, social and legal needs and aspirations is part of international diplomacy, including public diplomacy. Diplomacy appears as an area where international actors test, protect, develop and shape their identities and self-worth through diplomatic practices. Diplomatic interactions grounded on interest-based, value-based, relationship-based and right-based imperatives are affected by and affect diplomatic actors' sense of Self and collective self-regard. For diplomatic actors, a positive image of Self and self-respect are important for their effectiveness and emotional well-being but also have the practical reason of compelling others to see them positively. The most reliable way of forming a positive sense of Self is seeing significant Others' positive attitude toward Self. As symbolic interactionism underlines, self-concept and Other's view of Self are interdependent.

Diplomacy is rich with symbolism, its practice employs many symbolic means, including ceremonies and rituals. Diplomats represent their nations, and their behavior and intentions may symbolize their nations' behavior and intentions. Symbolic interaction plays an essential role in diplomacy and provides diplomatic actors with opportunities for both friendly and unfriendly actions toward each other.

Insult has no legitimate basis in international relations. But it exists as a social and political practice. Symbolic insult in diplomacy happens when one diplomatic actor misrecognizes the other one (diplomatic bypassing), or diplomatic actors enter direct confrontational interaction (diplomatic punch), or one of them inarticulately debases the opponent (diplomatic slap). Insult and humiliation can also happen accidentally or unintentionally, but usually actors do not take such incidents seriously. Apparently, an insulting intention and related act may not always lead to the actual insult: for this to happen, the targeted side should feel insulted. But the more hostile environment or competing political claims, the more opposing parties tend to see each other's opposing or challenging actions as insulting. Focusing on diplomatic actors' subtle, tacit and manipulative actions through the use of symbolic means, this paper states that symbolic insult in diplomacy aims to suppress or damage the opponent's sense of Self that is related to its identity, self-concept, integrity, dignity, honor, face, social status, reputation, core values and self-feeling. Symbolic insult in diplomacy appears to be a threat to the diplomatic actor's ontological security and can weaken the Self in confrontation with Other. It affects the victim's existential sense, its sense of being as a worthy and decent social actor. However, the ambiguity of unstated symbolic insult may allow the diplomatic actor to humiliate an opponent but at the same time to keep some level of working relationship. A diplomatic actor may take such an action when it tries to balance its interest-based and relationship-based imperatives, or political and social needs and aspirations. So, as a manipulative act, "diplomatic slap" or "diplomatic slap in the face" intends to defend or promote the actor's interests while keeping relationships with the opponent, although in a socially restructured, or hierarchical way. It also occurs as an instrument of concealed bargaining.

The practice of diplomatic symbolic insult evolved over time, and the most revealing in this sense is the emergence of the concealed digital insults. Diplomatic slap today may be quite different from those that existed in the past. But in terms of the "competent performance" or "efficiency", symbolic insult in diplomacy is defined by the "capacity" of advancing the insulter's interests while retaining its relationship with the insulted. As a part of the social game of diplomacy, symbolic diplomatic insult appears as an obscured expression of such a balancing, and also as one of the veiled and manipulative mechanism of counteracting Self and Other and their competing claims to status recognition.

Diplomatic actors are extremely sensitive to Self related matters, and may use such sensitivity for influencing each other, bargaining over the issues of importance, or simply defending their Selves while they confront the opponent. The diplomatic actor's acute sensitivity to recognition, honor and social status sharpens its sense of Self, and so makes any humiliation painful. In such a condition, protection of self-regard, dignity and face becomes a critical issue of diplomatic practice. At the same time, that makes a diplomatic actor's Self vulnerable and provides opponents opportunities for manipulations and symbolic abuse.

Symbolic insult and humiliation has a clear emotional attachment: insult hurts feelings, especially the sense of Self, oneness and integrity. But it also may represent political and social manipulative gamesmanship and calculated diplomatic strategy. Face-work, or face diplomacy, as we discussed, epitomizes these two sides of diplomatic symbolic insult: it is both an emotional and a strategic activity influenced by the public attention. Symbolic insult in diplomacy can happen behind closed doors, but the more expanded a circle of participants and observers of a diplomatic slap, the less limited its effect. In other words, when diplomacy is publicly staged, diplomatic actors tend to be more at risk of insult, and the insult can be felt stronger. The more publicly insult occurs, the more difficult to tolerate it.

Any insult, including a symbolic one, is negative: it hurts. Diplomatic insult appears as part of international politics and the existing disparity of political interests of different actors, or as a way of strategic interaction between conflicting parties as well as emotional reaction to the ontological threat. But paradoxically, sometimes symbolic insult may prevent diplomatic actors from committing a real war, i.e. to remain in the area of symbolic gamesmanship and not to step into the path of physical destruction of each other. However, it is important to work on the development of insult-free diplomacy—diplomacy that has a good-will and is truly about cooperation and problem-solving. In order to achieve that, we need to know the conditions for the emergence of diplomatic insults. Politicians, diplomats and the wider public need to understand the sensitivity and importance of the sense of Self and ontological security in diplomacy and international affairs as a whole. It is also important to analyze and discuss possible disparities between the diplomatic actor's different imperatives—clash of political and social motives, in case of symbolic insult—and the consequences of these. Diplomats need to detect any signs of symbolic insult and be able to work on the creation of common values and engage in meaningful symbolic interactions.

Social norms accepted in diplomatic protocol and etiquette are premeditated to exclude any symbolic offence of one diplomatic actor against another. Norms of international law are also designed to ensure equality of states and fairness in their relations. But existing international practices provide a certain social and reputational inequality for diplomatic actors in their real-world interactions, and opportunities for influencing each other, including by relational and symbolic means. However, because of high normativity of diplomatic behavior, even some small misuse or abuse of the accepted norms and protocol by visible politicians and diplomats in the international arena can be perceived by the public as an incident of a threat to Self.

Symbolic insult—lowering someone by hurting his or her sense of Self, integrity and status by symbolic means—can be both emotional and strategic act. It can be committed by the diplomatic actor as a reactive move to protect its ontological security and/or defend/elevate status as well as a proactive stroke to unbalance Other in order to promote its interests. In other words, it might be prompted by emotions or by strategic decision or based on both. Insulting someone might be a risky action because, as a reaction, the insulter can get a backfire—an insult, or face a more sophisticated revenge, or damage its relationship with the victim. By committing more delusive—symbolic—insult, diplomatic actor expects to gain an advantage, on the one hand, and keep relationship, on the other. So, symbolic insult by nature is a sophisticated manipulative act. But as any affective and damaging political action, insult may have different consequences, sometimes prolonged and unpredicted. Like in a chess game, even an advanced player may not know all the consequences of his or her moves. But international politics is far more complicated than any strategic board games, and playing with insult can be much more dangerous. However, when we deal with unintentional or non-deliberate insults in diplomacy, things are different: diplomatic actors try to consider them less seriously. But eventually many things depend on the interpretation of diplomatic signaling which is often ambiguous.

One of the ways of reducing diplomatic insults is the enhancing the role of value-based (moral), relationship-based (social) and right-based (legal) imperatives in diplomacy, and bonding actors' individual interest-based (political) imperatives with common inter-national interests. This is the way of developing more positive forms of diplomacy by transforming the Self's relations with Others, what Constantinou (2006) was writing about. Spreading best practices, compliance with diplomatic protocol and etiquette, regarding the high spirit of international diplomacy based on states' sovereign equality, reciprocity, respect, cooperation, consideration of mutual interests, search for peace, security, accord and friendly relations among nations, management of differences and conflicts through goodwill and finding common ground also acquire significance for avoiding insults in diplomacy.

As I pointed out, by symbolically insulting someone, the insulter can try to promote its political interests while maintaining normative relationships with the opponent. Symbolic insult also happens as a part of agreed international practices implicitly accepted by diplomatic actors within existing structures of power. In this sense, practice and habitus determine norms, and Bourdieu's theories of practice and symbolic violence may shed light on existing practices of symbolic insult in diplomacy. After all, symbolic insult in diplomacy is a violation of certain social norms and expectations. At the same time, as explored in this paper, an enormous importance of the collective sense of Self in diplomacy causes a variety of social strategic games, including symbolic insult, played by diplomatic actors, particularly in tacit bargaining and representational activities for affecting their counterparts' Selves as well as protecting their own self-regard, face and ontological security. That, in turn, affects the ways of conducting diplomacy and pre-mediates the absorption of symbolic insult in manipulative diplomatic practices. Paradoxically, therefore, diplomatic actors react to symbolic threat with indignation but nevertheless may use such a practice themselves. This can be compared with the social practice of deception: everyone knows that it is bad, but many social actors use it to achieve their objectives, sometimes even decent ones.

Practice and norms are interdependent: one creates the other. The same takes place in diplomatic practices and norms, including tacit practices and hidden norms existing in the processes of influence, persuasion, negotiation, bargaining and face-work. To reduce the use of symbolic insult in diplomacy, it is necessary to act on both sides—to change both the deceptive diplomatic practices and some of established norms. However, it is impossible to change the existing practices without changing the functioning norms, and to change the norms without changing practices. Therefore, a systemic or holistic approach, which has not yet been created, is needed.

References

ABC News (2017 a). "Donald Trump: Did the President just shove aside a prime minister?" 26 May. Available at: http://www.abc.net.au/news/2017-05-26/did-trump-just-shove-aside-a-prime-minister/8560830 (Accessed 25 October, 2017).

ABC News (2017 b). "Donald Trump: From Macron to Trudeau, relive the US President's handshakes". 15 July. Available at: http://www.abc.net.au/news/2017-07-15/donald-trump-emmanuel-macron-history-of-handshakes/8711314 (Accessed 14 August, 2017).

Adler-Nissen, Rebecca (2013). *Bourdieu in International Relation. Rethinking Key Concepts in IR*. London and New York: Routledge.

Adler-Nissen, Rebecca (2012). "Diplomacy as Impression Management: Strategic Face-Work and Post-Colonial Embarrassment", *Working paper 38, Centre for International Peace and Security Studies, McGill University and the Université de Montréal*. Montreal: McGill University.

Adler-Nissen, Rebecca (2011). "On a Field Trip with Bourdieu", *International Political Sociology* 5(3): 327–30.

Adler-Nissen, Rebecca (2014). "Stigma Management in International Relations: Transgressive Identities, Norms, and Order in International Society", *International Organization* 68(1): 143–176.

Adler-Nissen, Rebecca (2013). "Symbolic power in European diplomacy: the struggle between national foreign services and the EU's External Action Service", *Review of International Studies* 40(4): 657–681.

Allen, Nick, Oliphant, Roland and Foster, Peter (2016). "Donald Trump praises 'very smart' Vladimir Putin for not expelling US diplomats in response to sanctions", *The Telegraph*, 30 December. Available at: http://www.telegraph.co.uk/news/2016/12/29/obama-expels-35-russian-diplomats-election-hacking-row/ (Accessed on 26 July, 2017).

Alphand, Hervé (1977). *L'etonnement d'etre: Journal. 1939–1973*. Paris: Fayard.

Associated Press (2016). 13 February. "Russia's PM accuses West of rekindling Cold War", *New York Post*, February 13. Available at: http://nypost.com/2016/02/13/russias-pm-accuses-west-of-rekindling-cold-war (Accessed 27 August, 2017).

Arapov, Sherzod (2017). "The Use of Digital Diplomacy as a Tool for Symbolic Violence: Framing Analysis of Russian–Turkish Relations on Twitter", *Cambridge Journal of Eurasian Studies*, 1: #UZV32B, Available at: https://doi.org/10.22261/UZV32B (Accessed 3 August, 2017).

Armstrong, David (1993). *Revolution and World Order: The Revolutionary State in International Society*. New York: Oxford University Press.

Associated Press (2017). "President Trump Strikes Back at 'Short and Fat' Kim Jong Un", *Time*, 12November. Available at: http://time.com/5020694/donald-trump-kim-jong-un-twitter/ (Accessed 15 November, 2017).

Baczynska, Gabriela (2015). "Russia, Germany trade Cold War accusations", *Reuters*, 17 June. Available at: http://www.reuters.com/article/us-russia-nato-kremlin-idUSKBN0OX0XJ20150617 (Accessed 27 August, 2017).

Balmforth, Tom (2017). "As Ukraine Says 'Farewell Unwashed Russia,' Putin Says Take Care In 'Gay' Europe", 15 June. Available at: https://www.rferl.org/a/putin-unwashed-russia-poroshenko-ukraine-gay/28557438.html (Accessed 4 August, 2017).

Barnes, Joe (2017). "Trump grabs Macron for dominant handshake after French president makes bee-line for Merkel", *Express*, 26 May. Available at: http://www.express.co.uk/news/world/809350/Donald-Trump-Emmanuel-Macron-handshake-Nato-meeting-Angela-Merkel (Accessed 10 August, 2017).

Baker, Peter (2015). "Obama Set to See Putin, Though Both Deny Asking." *The New York Times*, September, 25. Available at: http://www.nytimes.com/2015/09/26/

us/politics/russia-says-putin-obama-meeting-was-american-idea.html (Accessed 2 February, 2017).

Barnes, Joe (2017). "Trump grabs Macron for dominant handshake after French president makes bee-line for Merkel", *Express*, 26 May. Available at: http://www.express.co.uk/news/world/809350/Donald-Trump-Emmanuel-Macron-handshake-Nato-meeting-Angela-Merkel (Accessed 10 August, 2017).

BBC News (1999 a). "Boris Yeltsin: Master of surprise". 31 December. Available at: http://news.bbc.co.uk/1/hi/world/europe/341959.stm (Accessed 6 August, 2017).

BBC News (2013). "Japan PM Shinzo Abe visits Yasukuni WW2 shrine". 26 December. Available at: http://www.bbc.com/news/world-asia-25517205 (Accessed 20 November, 2017).

BBC News (2017 a). "Nato meeting: Trump and Macron's awkward handshake in Brussels". 25 May. Available at: http://www.bbc.com/news/av/world-europe-40048008/nato-meeting-trump-and-macron-s-awkward-handshake-in-brussels (Accessed 10 August, 2017).

BBC News (2017 b). "Trump executive order: Million sign petition to stop UK visit". 30 January. Available at: http://www.bbc.com/news/uk-38795998 (Accessed 5 August, 2017).

BBC News (1999 b). "World: Europe Nato hits Chinese embassy", 8 May. Available at: http://news.bbc.co.uk/2/hi/europe/338424.stm (Accessed 23 September, 2017).

Berezhkov, Valentin (1993). *Kak ya stal perevodchikom Stalina*. Moskva: DEM. [In Russian].

Berlinger, Joshua and Wakatsuki, Yoko (2017). "Trump says 'all options on table' after North Korea fires missile over Japan", *CNN*, 30 August. Available at: http://edition.cnn.com/2017/08/28/politics/north-korea-launch-unidentified-projectile/index.html (Accessed 31 August, 2017).

Berne, Eric (1964). *Games People Play: The Psychology of Human Relationships*. New York: Grove Press.

Berthon, Simon and Potts, Joanna (2007). *Warlords: An Extraordinary Re-creation of World War II Through the Eyes and Minds of Hitler, Churchill, Roosevelt, and Stalin*. Boston, MA: Da Capo Press.

Blagburn, Francis (2017). "'Clasp, yank, release': the great Donald Trump handshake tracker", *The Telegraph*, 26 May. Available at: http://www.telegraph.co.uk/men/the-filter/clasp-yank-release-great-donald-trump-handshake-tracker/ (Accessed 15 August, 2017).

Blake, Aaron (2013). "Putin: America is not exceptional." *The Washington Post*, 12 September. Available at: http://www.washingtonpost.com/news/post-politics/wp/2013/09/12/putin-america-is-not-exceptional/ (Accessed 2 February, 2017).

Bially Mattern, Janice (2005). "Why 'Soft Power' Isn't So Soft: Representational Force and the Sociolinguistic Construction of Attraction in World Politics." *Millennium: Journal of International Studies* 33(3): 583–612.

Bially Mattern, Janice (2007). "Representational Force Meets 'Real'-ist Force Thoughts on the relationship between linguistic and material forms of coercion." *9ème Congrès de l'AFSP Toulouse/5–7 Septembre 2007*. Available at: http://www.afsp.msh-paris.fr/congres2007/tablesrondes/textes/tr6sess3biallymattern.pdf (Accessed 3 February, 2017).

Billing, Michael (1995). *Banal Nationalism*. London: SAGE Publications.

Bismarck (1898). *Bismarck. The Man and the Statesman. Being the Reflections and Reminiscences of Otto, Prince von Bismarck. Written and Dictated by Himself After His Retirement from Office*. Vol. 2. Translated from the German under the supervision of A. J. Butler. New York and London: Harper and Brothers.

Bjola, Corneliu (2013). "Understanding Enmity and Friendship in World Politics, The Case for a Diplomatic Approach", *The Hague Journal of Diplomacy* 8(1): 1–20.

Bjola, Corneliu and Kornprobst, Markus (2013). *Understanding International Diplomacy: Theory, Practice and Ethics*. Abingdon: Routledge.

Boyd, Gerald M. (1987). "Raze Berlin Wall, Reagan Urges Soviet", *The New York Times*, 13 June. Available at: http://www.nytimes.com/learning/general/onthisday/big/0612.html (Accessed 3 February, 2017).

Boyer, Dave (2016). "Putin snubs Obama, skips D.C. nuclear summit amid Islamic State fears", *The Washington Times*, 30 March. Available at: http://www.washingtontimes.com/news/2016/mar/30/russian-snub-mars-obamas-nuclear-summit-amid-isis-/ (Accessed 3 February, 2017).

Bourdieu, Pierre (2001). *Masculine Domination*. Translated by Richard Nice. Stanford, CA: Stanford University Press.

Bourdieu, Pierre (1977). *Outline of a Theory of Practice*. Translated by Richard Nice. Cambridge, UK: Cambridge University Press.

Braud, Philippe (2014). "Symbolic and Physical Violence", in *The International Politics of Recognition*, edited by Thomas Lindemann and Erik Ringmar. Boulder, CO and London: Paradigm Publisher, pp. 57–70.

Brummer, Alex (1987). "Mr Gorbachev, tear down this wall!", *Guardian, From the Guardian archive*, 13 June, 2012. Available at: http://www.theguardian.com/theguardian/2012/jun/13/archive-1987-reagan-gorbachev-berlin-wall (Accessed 3 February, 2017).

Bright, Martin (2004). "Gadaffi still hunts "stray dogs" in UK", *The Guardian*, 28 March. Available at: http://www.theguardian.com/uk/2004/mar/28/politics.libya (Accessed February 3, 2017).

Browning, Lynnley (2014). "Ambassador Tefft Would Upset Russia, and That's the Point." *Newsweek*, 14 May. Available at: http://www.newsweek.com/2014/05/23/

americas-ambassador-tefft-will-upset-russia-and-thats-point-251011.html (Accessed 3 February, 2017).

Bull, Hedley (2012). *The Anarchical Society: A Study of Order in World Politics*, 4th edn. Basingstoke: Palgrave Macmillan.

Burnett, Stephanie (2014). "Canada Trolls Russia on Twitter With Sardonic Geography Lesson", *Time*, 29 August. Available at: http://time.com/3218748/canada-trolls-russia-on-twitter-with-sardonic-geography-lesson/ (Accessed 8 August, 2017).

Burton, Neel (2014). "The Psychology of Humiliation: What is humiliation and can it ever be justified?", *Psychology Today*, 27 August. Available at: https://www.psychologytoday.com/blog/hide-and-seek/201408/the-psychology-humiliation (Accessed 27 May, 2017).

Business Insider (2017). "That time Putin brought his dog to a meeting to scare Angela Merkel", July 7, 2017. Available at: http://www.businessinsider.com/putin-merkel-meeting-dog-2017-7 (Accessed 31 July, 2017).

Cambon, Jules (1931). The Diplomatist. Translated by Christopher R. Turner. London: P. Allan.

Chandran, Nyshka (2016). "Donald Trump insults China with Taiwan phone call and tweets on trade, South China Sea", CNBC, 5 December. Available at: http://www.cnbc.com/2016/12/05/donald-trump-insults-china-with-taiwan-phone-call-and-tweets-on-trade-south-china-sea.html (Accessed 3 February, 2017).

Chappell, Bill (2017). "Macron's Strategy for Trump in Paris: Long Handshakes and Military Spectacles", NPR, 14 July. Available at: http://www.npr.org/sections/thetwo-way/2017/07/14/537210524/macrons-strategy-for-trump-in-paris-long-handshakes-and-military-spectacles (Accessed 17 August, 2017).

Cillizza, Chris (2017). "Donald Trump and Emmanuel Macron just exchanged a white-knuckled handshake", CNN, 26 May. Available at: http://edition.cnn.com/2017/05/25/politics/macron-trump-handshake/index.html (Accessed 16 August, 2017).

CNN Wire Service (2017). "North Korea vows to 'make the US pay dearly' as sanctions tighten". *Fox6Now*, 7 August. Available at: http://fox6now.com/2017/08/07/north-korea-vows-to-make-the-us-pay-dearly-as-sanctions-tighten/ (Accessed 8 August, 2017).

CNN Wire Service (2016). "Russia hits back at Pres. Obama with flurry of online insults", *Fox6Now*, 30 December. Available at: http://fox6now.com/2016/12/30/russia-hits-back-at-pres-obama-with-flurry-of-online-insults/ (Accessed 8 August, 2017).

Cohen, Raymond (1981). *International politics: The Rules of the Game*. London: Longman.

Cohen, Raymond (1987). *Theatre of Power: The Art of Diplomatic Signalling*. London and New York: Longman.

Conley, Thomas (2010). *Toward a Rhetoric of Insult*. Chicago and London: University of Chicago Press.

Constantinou, Costas (2016). "Everyday Diplomacy: Mission, Spectacle and the Remaking of Diplomatic Culture", in *Diplomatic Cultures and International Politics*, ed. Jason Dittmer and Fiona McConnell. London and New York: Routledge, pp. 23–40.

Constantinou, Costas M. (2006). "On Homo-Diplomacy", *Space and Culture* 9(4): 351–364.

Constantinou, Costas (1996). *On the Way to Diplomacy*. Minneapolis: University of Minnesota Press.

Constantinou, Costas and Der Derian, James (2010). "Sustaining Global Hope: Sovereignty, Power and the Transformation of Diplomacy", in *Sustainable Diplomacies*, edited by Costas M. Constantinou and James Der Derian. Basingstoke, UK and New York: Palgrave MacMillan.

Constantinou, Costas, Cornago, Noe and McConnell, Fiona (2016). "Transprofessional Diplomacy", *Diplomacy and Foreign Policy* 1(4): 1–66.

Cornago, Noé (2013). *Plural Diplomacies: Normative Predicaments and Functional Imperatives*. Leiden and Boston: Martinus Nijhoff Publishers.

Cornago, Noé (2015). "The Dead Body of the Diplomat", paper presented at the *EISA 9th Pan-European Conference of International Relations: The World of Violence*. Giardini Naxos, Sicily, 23–26 September 2015.

Cornut, Jérémie (2011). "An Eclectic Analysis of Apologies in U.S.-China Diplomacy", *Paper Prepared for the ISA Annual Conference*, Montreal, 16–19 March.

Cornut, Jérémie (2017). "Diplomacy, agency, and the logic of improvisation and virtuosity in practice", *European Journal of International Relations*, First Published September 8, https://doi.org/10.1177/1354066117725156.

Cornut, Jérémie (2009). "Pluralism in IR Theory: An Eclectic Study of Diplomatic Apologies and Regrets", *APSA 2009 Toronto Meeting Paper*. Available at SSRN: https://ssrn.com/abstract=1451684 (Accessed 23 September, 2017).

CNN Wire (2016). "Putin: Russia won't expel US diplomats", http://fox4kc.com/, 30 December. Available at: http://fox4kc.com/2016/12/30/putin-russia-wont-expel-us-diplomats/ (Accessed 26 July, 2017).

Cresci, Elena (2017). "Trump v Macron: French president appears to win latest handshake battle", *The Guardian*, 25 May. Available at: https://www.theguardian.com/us-news/2017/may/25/trump-v-macron-french-president-appears-to-win-latest-handshake-battle (Accessed 10 August, 2017).

Dejevsky, Mary (2017). "In defence of Donald Trump's Twitter diplomacy", *The Guardian*, 5 February. Available at: https://www.theguardian.com/commentisfree/2017/feb/05/in-defence-of-twitter-diplomacy (Accessed 8 August, 2017).

Der Derian, James (1987 a). "Mediating estrangement: a theory for diplomacy", *Review of International Studies* 13(2): 91–110.

Der Derian, James (1987 b). *On Diplomacy: A Genealogy of Western Estrangement*. Oxford: Basil Blackwell.

Deutsche Welle (2015). *"Tsipras plays the Russian Card"*. 8 April. Available at: http://www.dw.com/en/tsipras-plays-the-russian-card/a-18366308 (Accessed 10 September, 2016).

de Callières, François (2010). *On the Manner of Negotiating with Princes*. New York: Houghton Mifflin.

Dickson, Paul (2001). *Sputnik: The Shock of the Century*. New York: Walker & Company.

Dittmer, Jason and McConnell, Fiona, eds. (2016). *Diplomatic Cultures and International Politics: Translations, Spaces and Alternatives*. London and New York: Routledge.

Dyer, Geoff (2016). "Is Trump Using Taiwan as a China Bargaining Chip?", *Financial Times*, 6 December. Available at: https://www.ft.com/content/6f68c5a8-bb70-11e6-8b45-b8b81dd5d080 (Accessed 1 February, 2017).

Editorial Board (2017). "Meeting Putin was necessary—but hardly 'an honor'", *The Washington Post*, 7 July. Available at: https://www.washingtonpost.com/opinions/global-opinions/the-trump-putin-meeting-was-a-needed-first-step-for-the-worlds-major-nuclear-superpowers/2017/07/07/f92caafa-633d-11e7-8adc-fea80e32bf47_story.html?utm_term=.53a68b2f7599 (Accessed 5 August, 2017).

Encyclopædia Britannica (2014). "Ems telegram". Available at: https://www.britannica.com/event/Ems-telegram (Accessed 30 October, 2017).

Encyclopædia Britannica (1998). "William Pitt Amherst, 1st Earl Amherst". Available at: https://www.britannica.com/biography/William-Pitt-Amherst-1st-Earl-Amherst (Accessed 1 February, 2017).

Estepa, Jessica (2017). "President Trump shoved the Montenegro prime minister at NATO", *USA Today*, 25 May. Available at: https://www.usatoday.com/story/news/politics/onpolitics/2017/05/25/president-trump-shoved-montenegro-prime-minister-nato/102144808/ (Accessed 16 August, 2017).

Faizullaev, Alisher (2006). "Diplomacy and Self", *Diplomacy and Statecraft* 17(3): 497–522.

Faizullaev, Alisher (2013). "Diplomacy and Symbolism." *The Hague Journal of Diplomacy* 8(2): 91–114.

Faizullaev, Alisher (2014 a). "Diplomatic Interactions and Negotiations", *Negotiation Journal* 30(3): 275–299.

Faizullaev, Alisher (2007). "Individual Experiencing of States", *Review of International Studies* 33(3): 531–554.

Faizullaev, Alisher (2014 b). "Institutions and Culture in Regional Interactions and Negotiations: The Case of Central Asia", *Cambridge Central Asia Review* 1(1): 17–26.

Faizullaev, Alisher (2017). "Negotiating Security in Central Asia: Explicit and Tacit Dimensions", in *Tug of War: Negotiating Security in Eurasia*, edited by Fen Osler Hampson and Mikhail Troitskiy. Waterloo, ON, Canada: CIGI Press, pp. 163–181.

Faizullaev, Alisher (2015). "Symbolic Violence in International Negotiation and Bargaining", paper presented at the *EISA 9th Pan-European Conference of International Relations: The World of Violence*. Giardini Naxos, Sicily, 23–26 September 2015.

Faizullaev, Alisher and Cornut, Jérémie (2017). "Narrative Practice in International Politics and Diplomacy: the Case of the Crimean Crisis", *Journal of International Relations and Development* 20(3): 578–604.

Femenia, Nora (2000). "Emotional Actor: Foreign Policy Decision-Making in the 1982 Falklands/Malvinas War", in *Social Conflicts and Collective Identities*, edited by Patrick G. Coy and Lynne M. Woehrle. Lanham, MD: Rowman and Littlefield, pp. 41–65.

Fenton-Smith, Ben (2007). "Diplomatic condolences: ideological positioning in the death of Yasser Arafat", *Discourse and Society* (18)6: 697–718.

Firozi, Paulina (2017). "Martial arts academy posts how-to video for defending against Trump handshake", *The Hill*, 16 February. Available at: http://thehill.com/blogs/blog-briefing-room/news/319825-martial-arts-academy-posts-how-to-video-on-defending-against (Accessed 15 August, 2017).

Fisher, Roger and Ury, William with Patton, Bruce (1991). *Getting to Yes. Negotiating Agreement Without Giving In*, 2nd edn. New York: Penguin Books.

Folley, Aris (2017). "Emmanuel Macron appears to swerve Trump's handshake at NATO to hug Angela Merkel instead", *AOL.*, 26 May. Available at: https://www.aol.com/article/news/2017/05/26/emmanuel-macron-appears-swerve-trump-handshake-nato-hug-angela-merkel/22111118/ (Accessed 17 August, 2017).

Foreign Staff (2017). Emmanuel Macron swerves past Donald Trump to embrace Angela Merkel, *The Telegraph*, 26 May. Available at: http://www.telegraph.co.uk/news/2017/05/26/emmanuel-macron-swerves-past-donald-trump-embrace-angela-merkel/ (Accessed 10 August, 2017).

Freeman, Chas. W. Jr. (1997). *Arts of Power: Statecraft and Diplomacy*. Washington, DC: United States Institute of Peace Press.

Friedrichs, Jörg (2016). "An intercultural theory of international relations: how self-worth underlies politics among nations", *International Theory* 8(1): 63–96.

Giddens, Anthony (1991). *Modernity and Self-Identity: Self and Society in the Late Modern Age*. Stanford: Stanford University Press.

Glasser, Susan B. (2017). "The Shove Heard Round the World: How Donald Trump, Mitch McConnell and a Russian-backed coup attempt got tiny Montenegro into NATO", *Politico Magazine*, 12 June. Available at: http://www.politico.com/magazine/story/2017/06/12/the-shove-heard-round-the-world-215246 (Accessed 25 October, 2017).

Glavnoe (2015). "The Embassy of the Russian Federation called words of the head of the Polish Ministry of Agriculture 'grave sin' offensive". 11 August. Available at: http://en.glavnoe.ua/news/n237371 (Accessed 5 September, 2017).

Goffman, Erving (1967). *Interaction Ritual. Essays on Face-to-Face Behavior*. Garden City, NY: Doubleday.

Goffman, Erving (1959). *Presentation of Self in Everyday Life*. New York: Doubleday.

Goffman, Erving (1969). *Strategic Interaction*. Philadelphia, PA: University of Pennsylvania Press.

Goldberg, Geffrey (2016). "The Obama Doctrine." *The Atlantic*, April issue. Accessed February 5, 2017. http://www.theatlantic.com/magazine/archive/2016/04/the-obama-doctrine/471525/.

Gopnik, Adam (2017). "Emmanuel Macron's French Lessons for Donald Trump", *The New Yorker*, 25 May. Available at: http://www.newyorker.com/news/daily-comment/emmanuel-macrons-french-lessons-for-donald-trump (Accessed 10 August, 2017).

Gordon, Michael R. and Harris, Gardiner (2015). "Obama and Putin Play Diplomatic Poker Over Syria." *The New York Times*, 28 September. Available at: http://www.nytimes.com/2015/09/29/world/middleeast/obama-and-putin-clash-at-un-over-syria-crisis.html?_r=0 (Accessed 5 February, 2017).

Grinberg, Emanuella and Mortensen, Antonia (2017). "British PM to Russia: 'We know what you are doing'", *CNN*, 14 November. Available at: http://edition.cnn.com/2017/11/13/europe/theresa-may-russia/index.html (Accessed 14 November, 2017).

Hall, Rodney Bruce (2001). "Applying the 'Self/Other' Nexus in International Relations", *International Studies Review* 3(1): 101–111.

Hall, Todd (2015). *Emotional Diplomacy: Official Emotion on the International Stage. Ithaca*, NY: Cornell University Press.

Hansen, Lene (2015). "How images make world politics: International icons and the case of Abu Ghraib", *Review of International Studies* 41(2): 263–288.

Hansen, Lene (2006). *Security as Practice: Discourse Analysis and the Bosnian War*. London: Routledge.

Hansen, Lene (2011). "The politics of securitization and the Muhammad cartoon crisis: A post-structuralist perspective", *Security Dialogue* 42(4–5): 357–369.

Hartling, Linda M., Lindner, Evelin, Spalthoff, Ulrich, and Britton, Michael (2013). "Humiliation: A Nuclear Bomb of Emotion?", *Psicología Política* No 46: 55–76.

Head, Jonathan (2010). "Turkey threatens diplomatic action over Israel 'snub'", *BBC News*, 13 January. Available at: http://news.bbc.co.uk/2/hi/middle_east/8456804.stm (Accessed 5 February, 2017).

Hocking, Brian, Melissen, Jan, Riordan, Shaun and Sharp, Paul (2012). *Futures for Diplomacy: Integrative Diplomacy in the 21st Century*. The Hague: Netherlands Institute of International Relations "Clingendael".

Holmes, Markus (2013). "The Force of Face-to-Face Diplomacy: Mirror Neurons and the Problem of Intentions", *International Organization* 67(4): 829–861.

Honneth, Axel (1996). *The Struggle for Recognition. The Moral Grammar of Social Conflict*. Cambridge, MA: The MIT Press.

Hosie, Rachel (2017). "Donald Trump's Handshake: the Real Meaning explained by Body Language Expert", *Independent*, 14 February. Available at: http://www.independent.co.uk/life-style/donald-trump-handshake-meaning-justin-trudeau-shinzo-abe-explanation-body-language-expert-darren-a7579541.html (Accessed 15 August, 2017).

Hurd, Ian (2015). "Diplomacy and the Politics of International Law," in *Diplomacy and the Making of World Politics*, edited by Ole Jacob Sending, Vincent Pouliot, and Iver Neumann. Cambridge: Cambridge University Press, pp. 31–54.

Iovine, Anna (2017). "Psychologists break down the meaning of Donald Trump's handshake", *AOL*, 30 May. Available at: https://www.aol.com/article/news/2017/05/30/psychologists-break-down-the-meaning-of-donald-trumps-handshake/22116942/# (Accessed 15 August, 2017).

Inozemtsev, Vladislav (2017). "Diplomatichnyy" (Diplomatical). *Echo Moskvy*, 14 August. Available at: http://echo.msk.ru/blog/v_inozemcev/2036744-echo/ (Accessed 17 August 2017).

Jain, Sanya (2017). "The Evolution of the 'Donald Trump Handshake': A Study In GIFs", *NDTV*, 26 May. Available at: http://www.ndtv.com/offbeat/the-evolution-of-the-donald-trump-handshake-a-study-in-gifs-1704290 (Accessed 15 August, 2017).

Jennings, Ralph (2016). "Trump is Using Taiwan as a Bargaining Chip in Relations with China.' *Forbes*, 11 December. Available at: http://www.forbes.com/sites/ralphjennings/2016/12/11/trump-will-use-taiwan-as-a-bargaining-chip-in-relations-with-china/#2ed8bd565ee9 (Accessed 6 February, 2017).

Jönsson, Christer and Hall, Martin (2005). *Essence of Diplomacy*. Basingstoke and New York: Palgrave MacMillan.

Jönsson, Christer and Aggestam, Karen (1999). "Trends in Diplomatic Signalling", in *Innovation in Diplomatic Practice*, ed. Jan Melissen. Houndmills: Palgrave, pp. 151–170.

Jones, Shannon (2011). *Apology Diplomacy: Justice for All*? The Hague: Netherlands Institute of International Relations "Clingendael".

Kaplan, Fred (2009). "Handshake Diplomacy: What Obama's grip and grin with Hugo Chávez says about his foreign policy", *Slate*, 21 April. Available at: http://www.slate.com/articles/news_and_politics/war_stories/2009/04/handshake_diplomacy.html (Accessed 10 August, 2017).

Karagiannis, Emmanuel (2015). "Greece is not Russia's Trojan Horse to Europe", *Aljazeera*, 9 April. Available at: http://www.aljazeera.com/indepth/opinion/2015/04/greece-russia-trojan-horse-europe-150408121047432.html (Accessed 6 February, 2017).

Kaufman, Alison Adcock (2010). "The 'Century of Humiliation,' Then and Now: Chinese Perceptions of the International Order", *Pacific Focus* 25(1): 1–33.

Katz, Gregory (2016). "UK press up in arms over Obama comments about Cameron", *Associated Press and NewsOK.com*, 11 March. Available at: http://newsok.com/article/feed/980830 (Accessed February 7, 2017).

Kelsey, Adam (2017). "Trump and Macron cap first meeting with lengthy handshake", *ABC News*, 25 May. Available at: http://abcnews.go.com/Politics/trump-macron-cap-meeting-lengthy-handshake/story?id=47642123 (Accessed 10 August, 2017).

Kissinger, Henry (2011). *On China*. New York: The Penguin Press.

Klein, Aaron J. (2010). "Israel and Turkey: Anatomy of a Dissing War", *Time*, 14 January. Available at: http://content.time.com/time/world/article/0,8599,1953746,00.html (Accessed 7 February, 2017).

Klikushin, Mikhail (2017). "Putin Zings Obama With Vicious Historical Insult", *Observer*, 2 January. Available at: http://observer.com/2017/01/vladimir-putin-zings-barack-obama-over-anti-russian-sanctions/ (Accessed on 26 July, 2017).

Kheel, Rebecca and Mitchel, Ellen (2017). "Trump's diplomacy-by-Twitter sets off firestorm", *The Hill*, 6 June. Available at: http://thehill.com/policy/defense/336659-trumps-diplomacy-by-twitter-sets-off-firestorm (Accessed 8 August, 2017).

Korostelina, Karina V. (2014). *Political Insults: How Offenses Escalate Conflict*. New York: Oxford University Press.

Kroet, Cynthia (2017). "Support floods in for Montenegro PM after Trump shove", *Politico Magazine*, 6 June. Available at: http://www.politico.eu/article/donald-trump-nato-montenegro-pm-dusko-markovic-support-floods-in-for-after-shove/ (Accessed 16 August, 2017).

Kuch, Hannes (2011). "The Rituality of Humiliation: Exploring Symbolic Vulnerability", in *Humiliation, Degradation, Dehumanization: Human Dignity Violated*, edited by Paul Kaufman, Hennes Kuch, Christian Neuhäuser and Eliane Webster. Dordrecht: Springer, pp. 37–56.

Kuus, Merje (2014). *Geopolitics and Expertise: Knowledge and Authority in European Diplomacy*. London: Wiley Blackwell.

Langholtz, Harvey J. (2004). "The Psychology of Diplomacy", in *The Psychology of Diplomacy*, edited by Harvey J. Langholtz and Chris E. Stout. Westport, CT: Praeger, pp. 1–17.

Lanteigne, Marc (2013). "Commercial diplomacy: preferential trade agreements and soft power projection", in *China and the International System: Becoming a World Power*, edited by Xiaoming Huang and Robert G. Patman. London and New York: Routledge, pp. 71–88.

Le Miere, Jason (2017). "Who is the 'Bigger' man? Trump and Putin Handshake Will Bring 'an Olympian Level of Macho Posturing'", *Newsweek*, 3 July. Available at http://www.newsweek.com/trump-putin-handshake-machismo-meeting-631410?piano_t=1 (Accessed 29 July, 2017).

Lebow, Richard Ned (2008). *A Cultural Theory of International Relations*. Cambridge: Cambridge University Press.

Lederman, Josh and Vasilyeva, Nataliya (2016). "Putin says Russia won't expel US diplomats after all", *Associated Press for Boston Globe*, 30 December. Available at:

https://www.bostonglobe.com/news/world/2016/12/30/russia-will-expel-diplomats-response-obama-sanctions-report-says/satTpp7fmstHduCJZomFvI/story.html (Accessed on 26 July, 2017).

Lee, Matthew (2017). "Russia derides Tillerson statement on sanctions", *The Washington Post*, 29 July. Available at: https://www.washingtonpost.com/world/national-security/russia-derides-tillerson-statement-on-sanctions/2017/07/29/adb06538-7497-11e7-8c17-533c52b2f014_story.html?utm_term=.6d76f3c1e2e2 (Accessed 2 August, 2017).

Lendon, Brad and Berlinger, Joshua (2017). "Next target Guam, North Korea says", *CNN*, 31 August. Available at: http://edition.cnn.com/2017/08/29/asia/north-korea-missile-launch-guam-threat/index.html (Accessed 31 August, 2017).

Lindner, Evelin (2006). *Making Enemies: Humiliation and International Conflict*. Westport, CT and London: Praeger Security International.

Lindemann, Thomas (2010). *Causes of War: the Struggle for Recognition*. Colchester: ECPR Press.

Lindemann, Thomas and Ringmar, Erik, eds. (2014). *The International Politics of Recognition*. Boulder, CO and London: Paradigm Publishers.

Link, Taylor (2017). "Montenegro's prime minister didn't mind President Trump's shove seen round the world", *Salon*, 26 May. Available at: http://www.salon.com/2017/05/26/montenegros-prime-minister-didnt-mind-president-trumps-shove-seen-round-the-world/ (Accessed 9 August, 2017).

Litvinova, Daria (2015). "Putin Slams U.S. Refusal to Meet With Russian Delegation." *The Moscow Times*, 15 October. Available at: http://www.themoscowtimes.com/news/article/putin-slams-us-refusal-to-meet-with-russian-delegation/539191.html (Accessed 7 February, 2017).

Luhn, Alex (2017). "Russian embassy's Twitter account vents barbs against west", *The Guardian*, 12 April. Available at: https://www.theguardian.com/world/2017/apr/11/russian-embassys-twitter-account-vents-barbs-against-west (Accessed 7 August, 2017).

Manor, Ilan (2017). "Can Digital Diplomacy Really Start A War?", *Exploring Digital Diplomacy*, 21 August. Available at: https://digdipblog.com/2017/08/21/can-digital-diplomacy-really-start-a-war/ (Accessed 14 November, 2017).

Manor, Ilan (2015). "Framing Adversaries: Digital Diplomacy and Moral De-Legitimization", *Paper Presented at the 9th Pan-European Conference on International Relations September, 2015*. Available at: file:///Users/af/Downloads/Ilan%20Manor%20Framing%20Adversaries%20Digital%20Diplomacy%20and%20Moral%20De%20Legitimization.pdf (Accessed 20 November, 2017).

Manor, Ilan (2014). "How Governments Frame on Digital Diplomacy Channels", *Exploring Digital Diplomacy*, 14 July. Available at: https://digdipblog.com/2014/07/14/how-governments-frame-on-digital-diplomacy-channels/ (Accessed 12 November, 2017).

Mason, Rowena (2017). "Theresa May accuses Russia of interfering in elections and fake news", *The Guardian*, 14 November. Available at: https://www.theguardian.com/politics/2017/nov/13/theresa-may-accuses-russia-of-interfering-in-elections-and-fake-news (Accessed 14 November, 2017).

Maxwell, Robert Allan (2010). *Representing History, 900–1300: Art, Music*. University Park, PA: The Pennsylvania University Press.

Mazlish, Bruce and Weisbrode, Kenneth (2014). "Humiliation and Dignity in International Relations", *Diplomatic Courier*, 17 July. Available at: http://www.diplomaticourier.com/humiliation-and-dignity-in-international-relations/ (Accessed 7 February, 2017).

McCaskill, Nolan D. (2017). "Clinton slams Trump's Twitter diplomacy: 'That doesn't work'", *Politico*, 2 May. Available at: http://www.politico.com/story/2017/05/02/hillary-clinton-mocks-trump-twitter-diplomacy-237884 (Accessed 8 August, 2017).

McCauley, Clark (2017). "Toward a Psychology of Humiliation in Asymmetric Conflict", *American Psychologist*, 72(3): 255–265.

Mead, George Herbert (1934). *Mind, Self, and Society*. Chicago, IL: University of Chicago Press.

Meerts, Paul (1999). "The changing nature of diplomatic negotiation", in *Innovation in diplomatic practice*, edited by Jan Melissen. Basingstoke: Palgrave Macmillan, pp. 79–93.

Melissen, Jan (2005). "The New Public Diplomacy: Between Theory and Practice", in *The New Public Diplomacy Soft Power in International Relations*, edited by Jan Melissen. Basingstoke: Palgrave Macmillan, pp. 3–27.

Merriam-Webster Dictionary (2017). "Stratagem". Available at: https://www.merriam-webster.com/dictionary/stratagem (Accessed on 26 July, 2017).

Meyer, Henry and Arkhipov, Ilya (2017). "Russia Rues Trump-Putin Meeting That Got Away", *Bloomberg*, 13 November. Available at: https://www.bloomberg.com/news/articles/2017-11-13/russia-rues-trump-putin-meeting-that-got-away-as-rejection-hurts (Accessed 15 November, 2017).

Mindock, Clark (2017). "America's relationship with Russia at all-time low and deteriorating, says US Secretary of State", *Independent*, 13 June. Available at: http://www.independent.co.uk/news/world/americas/us-politics/us-russia-trump-putin-relationship-rex-tillerson-deteriorating-secretary-state-a7788076.html (Accessed 2 August, 2017).

Miller, Nick (2017). "'Getting it wrong could start a war': welcome to the age of digital diplomacy", *The Sydney Morning Herald*, 13 August. Available at: http://www.smh.com.au/world/getting-it-wrong-could-start-a-war-welcome-to-the-age-of-digital-diplomacy-20170810-gxtzt9.html (Accessed 20 November, 2017).

Mitzen, Jennifer (2006). "Ontological Security in World Politics: State Identity and the Security Dilemma", *European Journal of International Relations* 12(3): 341–370.

Moran, Lee (2017). "Emmanuel Macron Swerves Donald Trump To Hug Angela Merkel Instead", *Huffington Post*, 26 May. Available at: http://www.huffingtonpost.com/entry/macron-swerves-trump-merkel_us_5927ea41e4b06f608053826d (Accessed 10 August, 2017).

Morgenthau, Hans (1993). *Politics Among Nations. The Struggle for Power and Peace*, brief edn., rvsd by K. W. Thompson. New York: McGraw-Hill.

Nauert, Heather (2017). "Achieving Parity in Diplomatic Missions", *Press Statement of the U.S. Department of State*, 31 August. Available at: https://www.state.gov/r/pa/prs/ps/2017/08/273738.htm (Accessed 8 September, 2017).

Neu, Jerome (2008). *Sticks and Stones: The Philosophy of Insults*. New York: Oxford University Press.

Neumann, Iver B. (2012). *At Home with the Diplomats: Inside a European Foreign Ministry*. Ithaca, NY: Cornell University Press.

Neumann, Iver B. (2013). *Diplomatic Sites: A Critical Enquiry*. New York: Columbia University Press.

Neumann, Iver (1996). "Self and Other in International Relations", *European Journal of International Relations* 2(2): 139–174.

Neumann, Iver B. (2002). "The English School On Diplomacy", *Discussion Papers in Diplomacy*. The Hague: Netherlands Institute of International Relations "Clingendael".

Neumann, Iver and Pouliot, Vincent (2011). "Untimely Russia: Hysteresis in Russian-Western Relations over the Past Millennium", *Security Studies* 20(1): 105–137.

Nicholas, Peter (2009). "Obama defends greeting Hugo Chavez", *Los Angeles Times*, 20 April. Available at: http://www.latimes.com/la-fg-obama-americas20-2009apr20-story.html (Accessed 17 August, 2017).

Nicolson, Harold (1939). *Diplomacy*. London: Oxford University Press.

Oliphant, Ronald (2016). "Vladimir Putin denies setting his dog on Angela Merkel", *The Telegraph*, 12 January. Available at: http://www.telegraph.co.uk/news/worldnews/vladimir-putin/12094074/Vladimir-Putin-denies-setting-his-dog-on-Angela-Merkel.html (Accessed 31 July, 2017).

O'Neill, Barry (2001). *Honor, Symbols, and War*. Ann Arbor, MI: The University of Michigan Press.

Oxford Dictionaries (2017). Available at: https://en.oxforddictionaries.com/definition/self (Accessed 29 July 2017).

Palmeri, Tara (2017). "Trump slow to vet ultra-rich ambassador candidates", *Politico*, 15 January. Available at: http://www.politico.com/story/2017/01/trump-slow-to-vet-ultra-rich-ambassador-candidates-233631 (Accessed February 7, 2017).

Paipais, Vassilios (2011). "Self and Other in Critical International Theory: Assimilation, Incommensurability and the Paradox of Critique", *Review of International Studies* 37(1): 121–140.

Park, Madison (2013). "Yasukuni shrine visits: Japan honoring the dead or insulting the neighbors?", *CNN*, 26 December. Available at: http://edition.cnn.com/2013/10/21/world/asia/yasukuni-japan/index.html (Accessed 20 November, 2017).

Paul, T. V., Larson, Deborah Welch, and Wohlforth, William C., eds. (2014). *Status in World Politics*. New York: Cambridge University Press.

Plett Usher, Barbara (2016). "Is Taiwan a Bargaining-chip for Trump on China?", *BBC News*, 7 December. Available at: http://www.bbc.com/news/world-us-canada-38229654 (Accessed 7 February, 2017).

Pollmann, M. Erika (2016). "The Politics of Visiting the Yasukuni Shrine: Explaining Japanese Politicians' Behavior", *Georgetown Journal of Asian Affairs* 2(2): 123–152.

Porter, Tom (2017). "Emmanuel Macron Says Bone-Crushing Donald Trump Handshake Was 'Not Innocent'", *Newsweek*, 28 May. Available at: http://www.newsweek.com/macron-trump-616941 (Accessed 10 August, 2017).

Pouliot, Vincent (2011). "Diplomats as permanent representatives: The practical logics of the multilateral pecking order", *International Journal* 66(3): 543–561.

Pouliot, Vincent (2016). *International Pecking Orders: The Politics and Practice of Multilateral Diplomacy*. New York: Cambridge University Press.

Pouliot, Vincent (2010). *International Security in Practice: The Politics of NATO-Russia Diplomacy*. New York: Cambridge University Press.

Preza, Elizabeth (2017). "Internet cheers as French president beats Trump at his own 'bullsh*t macho handshake game'", *The Raw Story*, 25 May. Available at: http://www.rawstory.com/2017/05/internet-cheers-as-french-president-beats-trump-at-his-own-bullsht-macho-handshake-game/ (Accessed 10 August, 2017).

Putin, Vladimir V. (2013). "A Plea for Caution from Russia", *The New York Times*, 11 September. Available at: http://www.nytimes.com/2013/09/12/opinion/putin-plea-for-caution-from-russia-on-syria.html?_r=0 (Accessed 7 February, 2017).

Radchenko, Sergey (2016). "How Russian Blue Jeans Created a Diplomatic Incident in Mongolia", *The Diplomat*, 19 April. http://thediplomat.com/2016/04/how-russian-blue-jeans-created-a-diplomatic-incident-in-mongolia/?utm_content=buffer8e933&utm_medium=social&utm_source=twitter.com&utm_campaign=buffer (Accessed 7 February, 2017).

Radio Free Europe/Radio Liberty (2017). "Opponents of Montenegro Joining NATO Seize on Trump Shoving Incident". 27 May. Available at: https://www.rferl.org/a/opponents-montenegro-bid-join-nato-seize-on-trump-shoving-incident/28511844.html (Accessed 25 October, 2017).

Radio Poland (2015). "Agriculture Minister calls on Russia to halt food burning." 7 August. Available at: http://www.thenews.pl/1/10/Artykul/216457,Agriculture-Minister-calls-on-Russia-to-halt-food-burning (Accessed 5 September, 2017).

Ravid, Barak and the Associated Press (2010). "Peres: Humiliation of Turkey Envoy Does Not Reflect Israel's Diplomacy", *Haaretz*, 13 January. Available at: http://www

.haaretz.com/news/peres-humiliation-of-turkey-envoy-does-not-reflect-israel-s-diplomacy-1.261381 (Accessed February 7, 2017).

Renshon, Jonathan (2017). *Fighting for Status: Hierarchy and Conflict in World Politics*. Princeton, NJ: Princeton University Press.

Reus-Smit, Christian (1999). *The Moral Purpose of the state: Culture, social Identity, and Institutional Rationality in international Relations*. New Jersey: Princeton University Press.

Reus-Smit, Christian, ed. (2004). *The Politics of International Law*. Cambridge: Cambridge University Press.

Reuters (2017 a). "May says Queen invited Trump for state visit". 27 January. Available at: http://uk.reuters.com/article/uk-usa-trump-britain-queen-idUKKBN15B21U (Accessed 5 August, 2017).

Reuters (2017 b). "Trump, Macron engage in a little handshake diplomacy". 25 May. Available at: http://www.reuters.com/article/us-usa-trump-handshake-idUSKBN18L1OB (Accessed 10 August, 2017).

Reynolds, Paul (2010). "Snubs—part of the diplomatic game", *BBC News*, 14 January. Available at: http://news.bbc.co.uk/2/hi/in_depth/8456619.stm (Accessed 7 February, 2017).

RIA Novosti (2017). Peskov obyasnil sryv vstrechi Putina I Trampa na summite ATES". 12 November. Available at: https://ria.ru/politics/20171112/1508647631.html (Accessed 15 November, 2017).

Riker, William H. (1986). *The Art of Political Manipulation*. New Haven, CT: Yale University Press.

Riker, William H. (1995). "The Political Psychology of Rational Choice Theory", *Political Psychology* 16(1): 23–44.

Robbins, Helen Henrietta Macartney (2010). *Our First Ambassador to China*. Cambridge: Cambridge University Press.

Rogers, Katie (2017). "All the President's Handshakes", *The New York Times*, 15 July. Available at: https://www.nytimes.com/2017/07/14/us/politics/president-donald-trump-handshakes.html (Accessed 15 August, 2017).

Roth, Andrew (2017). "'Don't you look away from me!': How a Russian diplomat's tirade broke U.N. tradition", *The Washington Post*, 13 April. Available at: https://www.washingtonpost.com/news/worldviews/wp/2017/04/13/dont-you-look-away-from-me-how-a-russian-diplomats-tirade-broke-u-n-tradition/?utm_term=.f497019bddab (Accessed 7 August, 2017).

Rowling, J. K. (2017). Twitter Account. 25 May. Available at: https://twitter.com/jk_rowling/status/867794060525928448?lang=en (Accessed 25 October, 2017).

Rudolph, Harriet (2016). "Entangled Objects and Hybrid Practices? Material Culture as a New Approach to the History of Diplomacy", in *Material Culture in Modern*

Diplomacy from the 15th to the 20th Century, edited by Harriet Rudolph and Gregor M. Metzig. Berlin and Boston, MA: De Gruyter Oldenbourg.

Rudolph, Harriet and Metzig, Gregor M., eds. (2016). *Material Culture in Modern Diplomacy from the 15th to the 20th Century*. Berlin and Boston, MA: De Gruyter Oldenbourg.

Rumelili, Bahar (2015). "Identity and desecuritisation: the pitfalls of conflating ontological and physical security", *Journal of International Relations and Development* 18(1): 52–74.

RT (2017). "'Don't you dare insult Russia!': Moscow envoy chides UK counterpart at UNSC meeting". 12 April. Available at: https://www.rt.com/news/384540-russia-uk-envoy-unsc/ (Accessed 7 August, 2017).

RT (2014). "Geography can be tough indeed: Canada, Russia engage in tweet-for-tat war". 29 August. Available at: https://www.rt.com/news/183548-canada-geography-tweet-russia/ (Accessed 8 August, 2017).

Russian Foreign Ministry's Facebook page (2015). 8 September. Available at: https://www.facebook.com/MIDRussia/photos/a.265191980246917.43849.264205757012206/540729702693142/?type=1 (Accessed 8 August 2017).

Russian Foreign Ministry's Twitter page (2017). 14 November. Available at: https://twitter.com/mfa_russia/status/930424654858244096 (Accessed 15 November, 2017).

Saurette, Paul (2006). "You dissin me? Humiliation and post 9/11 global politics", *Review of International Studies* 32(3): 495–522.

Savic, Misha and Kuzmanovic, Jasmina (2017). "Trump Shove on Montenegro's Leader Draws Balkan Media Ire", *Bloomberg*, 26 May. Available at: https://www.bloomberg.com/news/articles/2017-05-26/trump-shove-on-montenegro-s-leader-sparks-balkan-media-rebuke (Accessed 16 August, 2017).

Schelling, Thomas (1980). *The Strategy of Conflict*. Cambridge, MA: Harvard University Press.

Schmidt, Samantha (2017). "Breaking down Trump's 'shove'", *The Washington Post*, 26 May. Available at: https://www.washingtonpost.com/news/morning-mix/wp/2017/05/26/breaking-down-trumps-shove-the-internet-debates-and-montenegros-leader-shrugs/ (Accessed 9 August, 2017).

Schmitt, Gary J. (2016). "Is Trump Using Taiwan as a Bargaining Chip with China?", *Newsweek*, 27 December. Available at: http://europe.newsweek.com/trump-using-taiwan-bargaining-chip-china-534394?rm=eu (Accessed 5 September, 2017).

Sending, Ole Jacob, Pouliot, Vincent, and Neumann, Iver B., eds. (2015). *Diplomacy and the Making of World Politics*. New York and Cambridge: Cambridge University Press.

Sennet, Richard (2012). *Together. The rituals, Pleasures and Politics of Cooperation* (Chapter "Everyday Diplomacy"). London: Penguin Books, pp. 211–246.

Sharp, Paul (2009). *Diplomatic Theory of International Relation*. Cambridge: Cambridge University Press.

Sharp, Paul (1999). "For Diplomacy: Representation and the Study of International Relations", *International Studies Review* 1(1): 33–57.

Sharp, Paul (2004). "The Idea of Diplomatic Culture and its Sources", in *Intercultural Communication and Diplomacy*, edited by Hannah Slavik. Malta and Geneva: DiploFoundation, pp. 361–379.

Shephard, Alex (2017). "Donald Trump's power handshakes are weird as hell", *New Republican*. Available at: https://newrepublic.com/minutes/140575/donald-trumps-power-handshakes-weird-hell (Accessed 5 September, 2017).

Siemaszko, Corky (2017). "Little Montenegro Muscles Way Into NATO, Despite Trump Shove", *ABC News*, 5 June. Available at: http://www.nbcnews.com/news/world/little-montenegro-muscles-way-nato-despite-trump-shove-n768376 (Accessed 16 August, 2017).

Sobczak, Pawel and John, Mark (2016). "Polish president Duda says Russia fomenting new Cold War", *Reuters*, 19 February. Available at: http://www.reuters.com/article/us-poland-president-nato-idUSKCN0VS1OZ (Accessed 5 September, 2017).

Sputnik (2017 a). "Big Men Need a Few Words: Trump-Putin 'Talk' Captured on VIDEO in Vietnam". 12 November. Available at: https://sputniknews.com/world/201711121059029467-putin-trump-talks-apec-summit/ (Accessed 15 November, 2017).

Sputnik (2017 b). "Kremlin Backs Russian UN Deputy Envoy's Harsh Speech in UN Security Council". 13 April. Available at: https://sputniknews.com/politics/201704131052598426-kremlin-un-envoy-speech-syria/ (Accessed 7 August, 2017).

Sputnik (2015). "Russian Prime Minister Blasts 'Foolish' US Decision to Skip Talks on Syria". 16 October. Available at: http://sputniknews.com/world/20151016/1028634661/Russia-US-Syria.html (Accessed 5 September, 2017).

Steele, Brent J. (2008). *Ontological Security in International Relations: Self-identity and the IR state*. London and New York: Routledge.

Stein, Sam (2017). "The Madness and Science Behind the Donald Trump Handshake", *Huffington Post*, 28 May. Available at: http://www.huffingtonpost.com/entry/donald-trump-handshake_us_592adb83e4b0df57cbfc23fd (Accessed 15 May, 2017).

Stratfor (2015). "Greece Uses Russia to Strengthen Its Position". 31 January. Available at: https://www.stratfor.com/analysis/greece-uses-russia-strengthen-its-position (Accessed 5 September, 2017).

Sun Tzu (2002). *The Art of War*. Translated by John Minford. New York: Penguin.

Symbolic Violence in Diplomatic Practice (2015). Section 52, 9th *Pan-European Conference on International Relations held in 23–26 November*, 2015, Giardini Naxos, Sicily, Italy. Available at: http://www.paneuropeanconference.org/2015/section.php?s=52 (Accessed on 28 July, 2017).

Suganami, Hidemi (2010). "The English School in a Nutshell", *Ritsumeikan Annual Review of International Studies* (9): 15–28.

Taylor, Adam (2017). "How the Russian Embassy in London uses Twitter to undermine the West", *The Washington Post*, 12 April. Available at: https://www.washingtonpost.com/news/worldviews/wp/2017/04/12/how-the-russian-embassy-in-london-uses-twitter-to-undermine-the-west/?utm_term=.00647cf69f82 (Accessed 7 August, 2017).

Taylor, Charles (1994). "The Politics of Recognition", in *Multiculturalism: Examining the Politics of Recognition*, edited by Amy Gutmann, 25–73. Princeton, NJ: Princeton University Press.

TASS Russian News Agency (2017 a). "Putin advises Ukraine's leadership to close off-shore accounts before becoming 'European'", 15 June. Available at: http://tass.com/politics/951457 (Accessed 4 August, 2017).

TASS Russian News Agency (2017 b). "Web users in Montenegro urge sanctions against US for incident with PM." 26 May. Available at: http://tass.com/world/947921 (Accessed 25 October, 2017).

Telegraph Reporters (2017). "Donald Trump shoves fellow Nato leader, the Montenegro PM, aside", *The Telegraph*, 25 May. Available at: http://www.telegraph.co.uk/news/2017/05/25/donald-trump-shoves-fellow-nato-leader-montenegro-pm-aside/ (Accessed 9 August, 2017).

The Conversation (2017). "The psychology behind Trump's awkward handshake … and how to beat him at his own game". 21 February. Available at: http://theconversation.com/the-psychology-behind-trumps-awkward-handshake-and-how-to-beat-him-at-his-own-game-73143 (Accessed 15 August, 2017).

The Economist (2014). "A slap in the face". 4 January. Available at: https://www.economist.com/news/asia/21592659-shinzo-abe-takes-dangerous-gamble-slap-face (Accessed 20 November, 2017).

The Economist (2001). "Insults and jitters in Cuba". 1 March. Available at: http://www.economist.com/node/518404 (Accessed 10 August, 2017).

The Economist (2016). "Taiwan Fears Becoming Donald Trump's Bargaining Chip". 17 December. Available at: http://www.economist.com/news/china/21711955-china-worries-about-president-elect-too-taiwan-fears-becoming-donald-trumps-bargaining-chip (Accessed 5 September, 2017).

The Ministry of Foreign Affairs of Russian Federation, website (2017). 28 July. Available at: http://www.mid.ru/en/web/guest/maps/us/-/asset_publisher/unVXBbj4Z6e8/content/id/2824435 (Accessed 4 August, 2017).

The Report of the Iraq Inquiry. Executive Summary (2016). Available at: http://www.iraqinquiry.org.uk/media/247921/the-report-of-the-iraq-inquiry_executive-summary.pdf (Accessed 7 September, 2017).

The Telegraph (2004). "Westerners struggle to scale the wall." 4 November. Available at: http://www.telegraph.co.uk/finance/2898668/Westerners-struggle-to-scale-the-wall.html (Accessed October 25, 2017).

The White House (2015). "Office of the Press Secretary, Press Briefing by Press Secretary Josh Earnest." 14 October. Available at: https://obamawhitehouse.archives.gov/the-press-office/2015/10/14/press-briefing-press-secretary-josh-earnest-10142015 (Accessed 5 September, 2017).

Thompson, Simon and Hoggett, Paul (2016). "Recognition and ambivalence", in *The Politics of Misrecognition*, edited by Simon Thompson and Majid Yar. Abingdon, Oxon: Routledge, pp. 17–32.

Thrush, Glenn and Bakeraug, Peter (2017). "Trump's Threat to North Korea Was Improvised", *The New York Times*, 9 August. Available at: https://www.nytimes.com/2017/08/09/us/politics/trump-north-korea.html (Accessed 31 August, 2017).

Tillerson, Rex W. (2017). "On Sanctions Legislation". *Press Statement, U.S. Department of State*. 29 July. Available at: https://www.state.gov/secretary/remarks/2017/07/272938.htm (Accessed 2 August, 2017).

Tisdall, Simon (2017). "Britain has a tradition of controversial state visits—Trump will fit in well", *The Guardian*, 30 January. Available at: https://www.theguardian.com/politics/2017/jan/30/donald-trump-state-visit-uk-controversial-tradition (Accessed 5 August, 2017).

Toosi, Nahal (2016). "Putin teases Kerry for carrying his own luggage." *Politico*, 24 March. Available at: http://www.politico.com/story/2016/03/putin-john-kerry-luggage-joke-221206 (Accessed 5 September, 2017).

Torbiorn, Ingemar (1982). *Living Abroad. Personal Adjustment and Personal Policy in the Overseas Settings*. Chichester: John Wiley and Sons.

Trianaphyllou, Dimitrios (2015). "The EU has reason to be concerned over relations between Greece and Russia." *LSE Europpblog*, 14 April. Available at: http://blogs.lse.ac.uk/europpblog/2015/04/14/the-eu-has-reason-to-be-concerned-over-relations-between-greece-and-russia/ (Accessed 5 September, 2017).

Tsygankov, Andrei (2012). *Russia and the West from Alexander to Putin: Honor in International Relations*. Cambridge: Cambridge University Press.

United States Diplomacy Center (2014). "Groundbreaking for the U.S. Diplomacy Center!". 3 September. Available at: http://diplomacy.state.gov/whatsnew/ (Accessed 7 February, 2017).

U.S. Department of State (2017). "Foreign Service Officer Qualifications—13 Dimensions". Available at: https://careers.state.gov/uploads/4c/e8/4ce8ce99d45087fc22dbd582ebab88f7/3.0.0_FSO_13_dimensions.pdf (Accessed 5 September, 2017).

Voeten, Erik (2011). "The practice of political manipulation", in *International Practices*, edited by Emanuel Adler and Vincent Pouliot. Cambridge, UK: Cambridge University Press, pp. 255–279.

von Senger, Harro (1993). *The Book of Stratagems: Tactics for Triumph and Survival*. New York: Penguin Books.

Wagner, Meg (2017). "Trump tells Brigitte Macron: 'You're in such good shape'", *CNN* Politics, 13 July. Available at: http://edition.cnn.com/2017/07/13/politics/trump-brigitte-macron-handshake/index.html (Accessed 10 August, 2017).

Walker, Shaun (2017). "Putin: Russia promises retaliation as Senate passes sanctions bill", *The Guardian*, 27 July. Available at: https://www.theguardian.com/world/2017/jul/27/putin-russia-us-sanctions-bill (Accessed 2 August, 2017).

Watson, Adam (1982). *Diplomacy: The Dialogue Between States*. London: Eyre Methuen.

Wawro, Geoffrey (2003). *The Franco-Prussian War The German Conquest of France in 1870–1871*. New York: Cambridge University Press.

Wendt, Alexander (1987). "The Agent-Structure Problem in International Relations Theory", *International Organization* 41(3): 335–370.

Wendt, Alexander (1999). *Social Theory of International Politics*. Cambridge: Cambridge University Press.

Wendt, Alexander (2004). "The state as person in international theory", *Review of International Studies* 30(2): 289–316.

Westcott, Ben (2017). "Chinese media to Trump: Stop the 'emotional venting' on Twitter", *CNN*, 2 August. Available at: http://edition.cnn.com/2017/08/02/asia/china-xinhua-trump-twitter/index.html (Accessed 8 August, 2017).

Wetzel, David (2001). *A Duel of Giants: Bismarck, Napoleon III, and the Origins of the Franco-Prussian War*. Madison, WI: The University of Wisconsin Press.

Williams, Michael C. (2007). *Culture and Security: Symbolic power and the politics of international security*. London, UK: Routledge.

Wingfield-Hayes, Rupert (2013). "Why Japan's Shinzo Abe went to Yasukuni shrine", *BBC News*, 26 December. Available at: http://www.bbc.com/news/world-asia-25518137 (Accessed 20 November, 2017).

Wiseman, Geoffrey (2010). "Engaging the Enemy: An Essential Norm for Sustainable US Diplomacy", in *Sustainable Diplomacies*, edited by Costas M. Constantinou and James Der Derian. Basingstoke, UK and New York: Palgrave MacMillan, pp. 213–234.

Wolf, Reinhard (2017). "Donald Trump's Status-Driven Foreign Policy", *Survival* 59(5): 99–116, DOI: 10.1080/00396338.2017.1375260. Available at: http://dx.doi.org/10.1080/00396338.2017.1375260 (Accessed 4 November, 2017).

Wolf, Reinhard (2011). "Respect and disrespect in international politics: the significance of status recognition", *International Theory* 3(1): 105–142.

Zhang, Hang (2001). "Culture and apology: The Hainan Island incident", *World Englishes* 20(3): 383–391.

Zakharova, Maria (2017). "Comment by Russian MFA Spokesperson Maria Zakharova on the anti-Russian statements by Theresa May", *The Ministry of Foreign Affairs of the Russian Federation*, 14 November. Available at: http://www.mid.ru/en/foreign_policy/news/-/asset_publisher/cKNonkJE02Bw/content/id/2949104 (Accessed 15 November, 2017).

Zartman, I. William and Berman, Maureen (1982). *The Practical Negotiator*. New Haven, CT: Yale University Press.

www.ingramcontent.com/pod-product-compliance
Lightning Source LLC
Chambersburg PA
CBHW031328230926
51848CB00001B/145
9789004354111